100 CLASSIC
CHINESE & THAI
RECIPES

100 CLASSIC
CHINESE & THAI
RECIPES

A TANTALIZING COLLECTION OF LOW-FAT DISHES FROM CHINA, THAILAND AND
SOUTH-EAST ASIA, ALL SHOWN STEP BY STEP IN MORE THAN 360 PHOTOGRAPHS

CONTRIBUTING EDITOR: JANE BAMFORTH

southwater

This edition is published by Southwater, an imprint of Anness Publishing Ltd, Hermes House, 88–89 Blackfriars Road, London SE1 8HA
tel. 020 7401 2077; fax 020 7633 9499

www.southwaterbooks.com; www.annesspublishing.com

If you like the images in this book and would like to investigate using them for publishing, promotions or advertising, please visit our website www.practicalpictures.com for more information.

UK agent: The Manning Partnership Ltd
tel. 01225 478444; fax 01225 478440; sales@manning-partnership.co.uk
UK distributor: Grantham Book Services Ltd
tel. 01476 541080; fax 01476 541061; orders@gbs.tbs-ltd.co.uk
North American agent/distributor: National Book Network
tel. 301 459 3366; fax 301 429 5746; www.nbnbooks.com
Australian agent/distributor: Pan Macmillan Australia
tel. 1300 135 113; fax 1300 135 103; customer.service@macmillan.com.au
New Zealand agent/distributor: David Bateman Ltd
tel. (09) 415 7664; fax (09) 415 8892

Publisher: Joanna Lorenz
Senior Managing Editor: Conor Kilgallon
Editors: Joy Wotton and Elizabeth Woodland
Recipes: Judy Bastyra, Jane Bamforth, Mridula Baljekar, Jenni Fleetwood,
Yasuko Fukuoka, Christine Ingram, Becky Johnson, Kathy Man,
Sallie Morris, Kate Whiteman
Home Economists: Annabel Ford, Becky Johnson, Lucy McKelvie,
Bridget Sargeson, Helen Trent
Photographers: Martin Brigdale, Nicky Dowey, Janine Hosegood, Becky Johnson,
Dave King, William Lingwood, Craig Robertson
Designer: Nigel Partridge
Production Controller: Wendy Lawson

© Anness Publishing Ltd 2008

Previously published as part of a larger volume, *Low-Fat, No-Fat Thai*

Main front cover image shows Morning Glory with Garlic and Shallots
– for recipe see page 100

Ethical Trading Policy

At Anness Publishing we believe that business should be conducted in an ethical and ecologically sustainable way, with respect for the environment and a proper regard to the replacement of the natural resources we employ.

As a publisher, we use a lot of wood pulp to make high-quality paper for printing, and that wood commonly comes from spruce trees. We are therefore currently growing more than 500,000 trees in two Scottish forest plantations near Aberdeen – Berrymoss (130 hectares/320 acres) and West Touxhill (125 hectares/305 acres). The forests we manage contain twice the number of trees employed each year in paper-making for our books.

Because of this ongoing ecological investment programme, you, as our customer, can have the pleasure and reassurance of knowing that a tree is being cultivated on your behalf to naturally replace the materials used to make the book you are holding. Our forestry programme is run in accordance with the UK Woodland Assurance Scheme (UKWAS) and will be certified by the internationally recognized Forest Stewardship Council (FSC). The FSC is a non-government organization dedicated to promoting responsible management of the world's forests. Certification ensures forests are managed in an environmentally sustainable and socially responsible way. For further information about this scheme, go to www.annesspublishing.com/trees

Notes

Bracketed terms are intended for American readers.
For all recipes, quantities are given in both metric and imperial measures and, where appropriate, in standard cups and spoons. Follow one set, but not a mixture, because they are not interchangeable.
Standard spoon and cup measures are level.
1 tsp = 5ml, 1 tbsp = 15ml, 1 cup = 250ml/8fl oz.
Australian standard tablespoons are 20ml. Australian readers should use 3 tsp in place of 1 tbsp for measuring small quantities of gelatine, flour, salt, etc.
American pints are 16fl oz/2 cups. American readers should use 20fl oz/2.5 cups in place of 1 pint when measuring liquids.
Electric oven temperatures in this book are for conventional ovens. When using a fan oven, the temperature will probably need to be reduced by about 10–20°C/20–40°F. Since ovens vary, you should check with your manufacturer's instruction book for guidance.
The nutritional analysis given for each recipe is calculated per portion (i.e. serving or item), unless otherwise stated. If the recipe gives a range, such as Serves 4–6, then the nutritional analysis will be for the smaller portion size, i.e. 6 servings. Measurements for sodium do not include salt added to taste.
Medium (US large) eggs are used unless otherwise stated.

Each recipe title is followed by a symbol that indicates the following:
★ = 5g of fat or less per serving
★★ = 10g of fat or less per serving
★★★ = 15g of fat or less per serving

CONTENTS

INTRODUCTION

The food of China, Thailand and South-east Asia is a joy to the senses, combining the refreshing aroma of lemon grass and kaffir lime leaves with the pungency of brilliant red chillies and the magical flavours of coconut milk and fresh basil. South-east Asian curries are very different from their Indian counterparts: Indian curries are traditionally slow-cooked for a rich, creamy taste, while South-east Asian dishes are famously quick and easy to prepare.

Exotic cuisines are increasingly popular in the West, and enthusiastic cooks are keen to reproduce them in their own kitchens. This book, with its extensive and wide-ranging collection of recipes from all over South-east Asia, will supply delicious ideas for new gastronomic discoveries.

China and Thailand is a great source of healthy, low-fat recipes. Asian cooks are fussy about what they eat, and ingredients are chosen with considerable care. Visit any open-air market and you will see cooks sifting through piles of gourds to choose one that is at just the right state of ripeness for the meal they have planned. Meat and fish must be very fresh, a fact that can be a bit daunting to the visitor invited to choose their meal while the fish is still swimming in a tank, but this is a method which proves beyond any doubt that the item in question will not have far to travel to their table.

A HEALTHY WAY OF COOKING

The majority of people living in South-east Asia have a very healthy diet, which is low in fat, high in fibre, with plenty of vegetables and relatively small amounts of meat. Much of their protein comes from fish and tofu, both of which are low-fat foods. Noodles and rice form the bulk of most meals, and processed foods are seldom eaten. In part, this diet evolved through necessity. Subsistence workers could not afford to eat large quantities of meat on a daily basis, even though pork, duck and chicken were – and still remain – an important part of the diet.

Steaming and stir-frying are two of the most popular cooking methods South-east Asia. Both these methods are ideal for the low-fat cook, since they require little or no oil to be used. The wok is the principal utensil. This extraordinarily versatile pan, with its rounded bottom, was originally designed to fit snugly on a traditional Asian brazier or stove. Modern versions have flatter bases, to prevent wobble on electric stoves, but are still very efficient in the even way they conduct and retain heat. The sloping sides mean that the food always returns to the centre, where the heat is most intense.

Many of the woks on sale today are non-stick. Although traditional carbonized steel woks are the ones purists choose, because they are so efficient, non-stick woks are better for low-fat cooking, since they make it possible to stir-fry with the smallest amount of oil.

When stir-frying, the best technique is to place the wok over the heat without any oil. When the pan is hot, dribble drops of oil, necklace fashion, on to the inner surface just below the rim. As the drops slither down the pan, they coat the sides, then puddle on the base. You can get away with using just about a teaspoon of oil if you follow this method. Add the food to be cooked when the oil is very hot, and keep it moving with a pair of chopsticks or two spatulas or spoons.

Left: Noodles add bulk and extra flavour to dishes without having a significant impact on fat levels. Fresh or dried egg noodles are available in various widths.

Above: Tiny bird's eye chillies are thin-fleshed and very hot. They give many Thai dishes their characteristic fiery flavour without adding any fat to the finished dish.

Add a metal trivet to a wok and it becomes a steamer. Better still, use a bamboo steamer. These attractive-looking utensils look rather like hat boxes, and come with tightly fitting domed lids. You can stack several tiers on top of each other over a wok partly filled with water. No fat will be needed and the food will taste delicious, with just a hint of fragrance from the bamboo.

A HEALTHY LIFESTYLE

Most of us eat fats in some form or another every day and we all need a small amount of fat in our diet to maintain a healthy, balanced eating plan. However, many of us eat far too much fat, and we should all be looking to reduce our overall fat intake, especially of saturated fats, and choose the healthier unsaturated fats.

Regular exercise is also an important factor in a healthy lifestyle, and we should all be aiming to exercise three times a week for a minimum of half an hour each session. Swimming, brisk walking, jogging, dancing, skipping and cycling are all good forms of aerobic exercise promoting a healthy heart.

ABOUT THIS BOOK

From many regions of China, Thailand and South-east Asia, this cookbook brings together a wide selection of delicious and nutritious dishes, all of which are low in fat, and are ideal to include as part of an everyday healthy and low-fat eating plan.

The book includes plenty of useful and informative advice. A succinct introduction gives a blueprint for healthy eating and has helpful hints and tips on low-fat and fat-free ingredients and cooking techniques. There are plenty of practical tips for reducing fat, especially saturated fat, in your diet, and there is a useful guide to calorie contents to the typical foods used in Chinese and Thai cooking.

The tempting recipes – all 100 of them – will be enjoyed by the whole family. They range from soups and appetizers to desserts and there are lots of delicious main course dishes for meat eaters and vegetarians. The emphasis throughout the book is on good food with maximum taste, and if you don't let on that the dishes are also low in fat, nobody is likely to guess.

THE LOW-FAT RECIPES

Each recipe includes a nutritional breakdown, proving an at-a-glance guide to calorie and fat content (including saturates and polyunsaturates content) per serving, as well as other key components such as protein, carbohydrate, calcium, cholesterol, fibre and sodium. All the recipes in this collection are low in fat. Many contain

Above: Dry and wet spices, aromatics and herbs are often pounded together to form spice pastes. Strong-tasting shrimp paste may be added.

less than five grams of total fat per serving, and a few are even lower in fat, with under one gram per serving. One or two classic recipes, such as Chicken Satay with Peanut Sauce and Stir-fried Beef in Oyster Sauce, contain slightly more fat, but even these contain less than in the traditional versions.

For ease of reference, all recipes with a single * after the recipe title contain a maximum of five grams of total fat, those with ** contain a maximum of 10 grams of total fat and those with *** contain up to 15 grams of total fat per portion. Each recipe also has a complete breakdown of the energy, protein, carbohydrate, cholesterol, calcium, fibre and sodium values of the food.

Although the recipes are low in fat, they lose nothing in terms of flavour. This practical cookbook will enable you to enjoy healthy Chinese, Thai and South-east Asian food with a clear conscience. All the recipes are easy to cook and many are so quick that you'll have supper on the table in less time than it would have taken to collect a take-away.

Left: Woks may have flat or rounded bases and one or two handles.

PLANNING A LOW-FAT DIET

Cutting down on fat on an everyday basis means we need to keep a close eye on the fat content of everything we eat. These general guidelines on reducing fat are applicable to all cuisines.

CUTTING DOWN ON FAT IN THE DIET

Most of us eat far more fat than we require – consuming about 115g/4oz of fat every day. Yet just 10g/¼oz, the amount in a single packet of crisps (US potato chips) or a thin slice of cheese, is all that we actually need.

Current nutritional thinking is more lenient than this and suggests an upper daily limit of about 70g/2¾oz total fat.

Using low-fat recipes helps to reduce the overall daily intake of fat, but there are also lots of other ways of reducing the fat in your diet. Just follow the "eat less, try instead" suggestions below to discover how easy it can be.

• Eat less butter, margarine, other spreading fats and cooking oils. Try reduced-fat spreads, low-fat spreads or fat-free spreads. Butter or hard margarine should be softened at room temperature so that they can be spread thinly. Try low-fat cream cheese or low-fat soft cheese for sandwiches and toast.

• Eat less full-fat dairy products such as whole milk, cream, butter, hard margarine, crème fraîche, whole-milk yogurts and hard cheese. Try instead semi-skimmed (low-fat) or skimmed milk, low-fat or reduced-fat milk products, such as low-fat yogurts and soft cheeses, reduced-fat hard cheeses such as Cheddar, and reduced-fat crème fraîche.

• Silken tofu can be used instead of cream in soups and sauces. It is a good source of calcium and an excellent protein food.

• Eat fewer fatty cuts of meat and high-fat meat products, such as pâtés, burgers, pies and sausages. Try instead naturally low-fat meats such as skinless chicken and turkey, ostrich and venison. When cooking lamb, beef or pork, use only the leanest cuts. Always cut away any visible fat and skin from meat before cooking. Try substituting low-fat protein ingredients like dried beans, lentils or tofu for some or all of the meat in a recipe.

• Eat more fish. It is easy to cook, tastes great, and if you use a steamer, you won't need to add any extra fat at all.

• Eat fewer hard cooking fats, such as lard or hard margarine. Try instead polyunsaturated or monounsaturated oils, such as sunflower or corn oil, and don't use too much.

• Eat fewer rich salad dressings and less full-fat mayonnaise. Try reduced-fat or fat-free dressings, or just a squeeze of lemon juice. Use a reduced-fat mayonnaise and thin it with puréed silken tofu for an even greater fat saving.

• Eat less fried food. Try fat-free cooking methods like steaming, grilling (broiling), baking or microwaving. Use non-stick pans with spray oil. When roasting or grilling meat, place it on a rack and drain off excess fat frequently.

• Eat fewer deep-fried or sautéed potatoes. Boil or bake them instead, or use other carbohydrates. Avoid chow-mein noodles, which are high in fat.

Above: Tuna and salmon are good sources of Omega-3 fatty acids, so although they do contain some fat, it's a beneficial variety.

• Cut down on oil when cooking. Drain fried food on kitchen paper to remove as much oil as possible. Choose heavy, good-quality non-stick pans and use spray oil for the lightest coverage. Moisten food with fat-free or low-fat liquids such as fruit juice, defatted stock, wine or even beer.

• Eat fewer high-fat snacks, such as chocolate, cookies, chips (French fries) and crisps. Try instead a piece of fruit, some vegetable crudités or some home-baked low-fat fruit cake.

Below: Choose lean cuts of meat and naturally low-fat meats such as skinless chicken and turkey.

Above: For fat-free snacks that are always available, keep a supply of exotic fresh fruit to hand including star fruit (carambola), papaya and lychees.

FAT-FREE COOKING METHODS

Chinese, Thai and South-east Asian cooking uses a variety of low-fat cooking methods, and by incorporating recipes from this region into your daily diet it is easy to bring down your total fat consumption. Where possible, steam, microwave or grill (broil) foods, without adding extra fat. Alternatively, braise in a defatted stock, wine or fruit juice, or stir-fry with just a spray of vegetable oil.

• By choosing a good quality, non-stick wok, such as the one above, you can keep the amount of fat needed for cooking foods to the absolute minimum. When cooking meat in a regular pan, dry-fry the meat to brown it, then tip it into a sieve (strainer) and drain off the excess fat before returning it to the pan and adding the other ingredients. If you do need a little fat for cooking, choose an oil high in unsaturates, such as sunflower or corn oil and use a spray where possible.

• Eat less meat and more vegetables and noodles or other forms of pasta. A good method for making a small amount of meat such as beef steak go a long way is to place it in the freezer for 30 minutes and then slice it very thinly with a sharp knife. Meat prepared this way will cook very quickly with very little fat.

• When baking chicken or fish, wrap it in a loose package of foil or baking parchment, with a little wine or fruit juice. Add some fresh herbs or spices before sealing the parcel, if you like.

• It is often unnecessary to add fat when grilling (broiling) food. If the food shows signs of drying, lightly brush or spray it with a little unsaturated oil, such as sunflower, corn or olive oil. Microwaved foods seldom need the addition of fat, so add herbs or spices for extra flavour and colour.

• Steaming is the ideal way of cooking fish. If you like, arrange the fish on a bed of aromatic flavourings such as lemon or lime slices and sprigs of herbs. Alternatively, place finely shredded vegetables or seaweed in the base of the steamer to give the fish extra flavour.

• If you do not own a steamer, cook vegetables in a covered pan over low heat with just a little water, so that they cook in their own juices.
• Vegetables can be braised in the oven in low-fat or fat-free stock, wine or a little water with some chopped fresh or dried herbs.
• Try poaching foods such as chicken, fish or fruit in low-fat or fat-free stock or fruit juice.
• Plain rice or noodles make a very good low-fat accompaniment to most Thai and South-east Asian dishes.

• The classic Asian technique of adding moisture and flavour to chicken by marinating it in a mixture of soy sauce and rice wine, with a little sesame oil, can be used with other meats too. You can also use a mixture of alcohol, herbs and spices, or vinegar or fruit juice. The marinade will also help to tenderize the meat and any remaining marinade can be used to baste the food while it is cooking.
• When serving vegetables, resist the temptation to add butter. Instead, sprinkle with chopped fresh herbs.

Low-fat spreads in cooking
A huge variety of low-fat and reduced-fat spreads is available in supermarkets, along with some spreads that are very low in fat. Generally speaking, any very low-fat spreads with a fat content of around 20 per cent or less have a high water content. These are unsuitable for cooking and can only be used for spreading.

FAT AND CALORIE CONTENTS OF FOOD

The figures show the weight of fat (g) and the energy content per 100g (3½oz) of each of the following typical foods used in Chinese, Thai and South-east Asian cooking. Use the table to help work out the fat content of favourite dishes.

MEATS	fat (g)	Energy kcals/kJ
Beef minced (ground), raw	16.2	225kcal/934kJ
Beef, rump (round) steak, lean only	4.1	125kcal/526kJ
Beef, fillet (tenderloin) steak	8.5	191kcal/799kJ
Chicken, minced (ground), raw	8.5	106kcal/449kJ
Chicken fillet, raw	1.1	106kcal/449kJ
Chicken thighs, without skin, raw	6.0	126kcal/530kJ
Duck, without skin, cooked	9.5	182kcal/765kJ
Lamb leg, lean, cooked	6.3	198kcal/831kJ
Liver, lamb's, raw	6.2	137kcal/575kJ
Pork, average, lean, raw	4.0	123kcal/519kJ
Pork, lean roast	4.0	163kcal/685kJ
Pork, minced (ground), raw	4.0	123kcal/519kJ
Pork, ribs, raw	10.0	114kcal/480kJ
Turkey, meat only, raw	1.6	105kcal/443kJ
Turkey, minced (ground), raw	6.5	170kcal/715kJ

FISH AND SHELLFISH	fat (g)	Energy kcals/kJ
Cod, raw	0.7	80kcal/337kJ
Crab meat, raw	0.5	54kcal/230kJ
Mackerel, raw	16.0	221kcal/930kJ
Monkfish, raw	1.5	76kcal/320kJ
Mussels, raw, weight without shells	1.8	74kcal/312kJ
Mussels, raw, weight with shells	0.6	24kcal/98kJ
Oysters, raw	4.2	120kcal/508kJ
Prawns (shrimp)	1.0	76kcal/320kJ
Salmon, steamed	13.0	200kcal/837kJ
Scallops, raw	1.6	105kcal/440kJ
Sardine fillets, grilled	10.4	195kcal/815kJ
Sardines, grilled, weight with bones	6.3	19kcal/497kJ
Sea bass, raw	2.0	97kcal/406kJ
Squid, boiled	1.0	79kcal/330kJ
Swordfish, grilled	5.1	155kcal/649kJ
Tuna, grilled	6.3	184kcal/770kJ

VEGETABLES	fat (g)	Energy kcals/kJ
Asparagus	0.0	12.5kcal/52.5kJ
Aubergine (eggplant)	0.4	15kcal/63kJ
Bamboo shoots	0.0	29kcal/120kJ
Beansprouts	1.6	10kcal/42kJ
(Bell) peppers	0.4	32kcals/128kJ
Beans, fine green	0.0	7kcal/29kJ
Beetroot (beets)	0.1	36kcal/151kJ
Broccoli	0.9	33kcal/138kJ
Carrot	0.3	35kcal/156kJ
Celery	0.2	7kcal/142kJ
Chilli, fresh	0.0	30kcal/120kJ
Chinese leaves (Chinese cabbage)	0.0	8kcal/35kJ
Courgettes (zucchini)	0.4	18kcal74kJ
Cucumber	0.1	10kcal/40kJ
Leek	0.3	20kcal/87kJ
Lotus root, raw	0.0	74kcal/310kJ
Mangetouts (snow peas)	0.4	81kcal/339kJ
Mung beans, cooked	0.1	70kcal/295kJ
Mushrooms, button (white)	0.5	24kcal/100kJ
Mushrooms, shiitake	0.2	55kcal/230kJ
Mushrooms, dried	0.0	56kcal/240kJ
Onion	0.2	36kcal/151kJ
Pak choi (bok choy)	0.0	13kcal/53kJ
Spinach (fresh, cooked)	0.0	20kcal/87kJ
Spring onion (scallion)	0.0	17kcal/83kJ
Sweet potato (peeled, boiled)	0.0	84kcal/358kJ
Water chestnuts	0.0	98kcal/410kJ

NUTS AND SEEDS	fat (g)	Energy kcals/kJ
Cashew nuts	48.0	573kcal/2406kJ
Chestnuts	2.7	169kcal/714kJ
Peanuts	26.9	586kcal/2464kJ
Sesame seeds	47.0	507kcal/2113kJ

Below: Red meat such as beef, lamb and pork have a higher quantity of fat per 100g than white meat.

Below: Seafood is a good source of vitamins, minerals and protein. Oily fish contains high levels of Omega-3 fatty acids.

FRUIT	fat (g)	Energy kcals/kJ
Apples, eating	0.1	47kcal/199kJ
Bananas	0.3	95kcal/403kJ
Grapefruit	0.1	30kcal/126kJ
Grapes (green)	0.0	56kcal/235kJ
Lychees	0.1	58kcal/248kJ
Mangoes	0.0	60Kcal/251kJ
Nectarine	0.0	40kcal/169kJ
Oranges	0.1	37kcal/158kJ
Papayas	0.0	36kcal/153kJ
Peaches	0.0	31kcal/132kJ
Pineapple, fresh	0.0	50Kcal/209kJ
Pineapple, canned chunks	0.2	63Kcal/264kJ
Raspberries	0.0	28Kcal/117kJ
Star fruit (carambola)	0.0	25Kcal/105kJ
Strawberries	0.0	27kcal/113kJ
Watermelon	0.0	23kcal/95kJ

BEANS, NOODLES, RICE AND TOFU		
Aduki beans, cooked	0.2	123kcal/525kJ
Noodles, cellophane	trace	351kcal/1468kJ
Noodles, egg	0.5	62kcal/264kJ
Noodles, plain wheat	2.5	354kcal/1190kJ
Noodles, rice	0.1	360kcal/1506kJ
Noodles, soba	0.1	99kcal/414kJ
Rice, brown, uncooked	2.8	357kcal/1518kJ
Rice, white, uncooked	3.6	383kcal/1630kJ
Tofu, firm	4.2	73kcal/304kJ
Tofu, silken	2.5	55kcal/230kJ

BAKING AND PANTRY		
Cornflour (cornstarch)	0.7	354kcal/1508kJ
Flour, plain (all-purpose) white	1.3	341kcal/1450kJ
Flour, self-raising (self-rising)	1.2	330kcal/1407kJ
Flour, wholemeal (whole-wheat)	2.2	310kcal/1318kJ
Tapioca	0.0	28kcal/119kJ
Honey	0.0	288kcal/1229kJ
Soy sauce, per 5ml/1 tsp	0.0	9kcal/40kJ
Sugar, white	0.3	94kcal/1680kJ

FATS, OILS AND EGGS	fat (g)	Energy kcals/kJ
Butter	81.7	737kcal/3031kJ
Low-fat spread	40.5	390kcal/1605kJ
Very low-fat spread	25.0	273kcal/1128kJ
Oil, corn, per 1 tbsp/15ml	13.8	124kcal/511kJ
Oil, groundnut (peanut), per 1 tbsp/15ml	14.9	134kcal/552kJ
Oil, sesame seed, per 1 tbsp/15ml	14.9	134kcal/552kJ
Oil, sunflower, per 1 tbsp/15ml	13.8	124kcal/511kJ
Eggs	10.8	147kcal/612kJ
Coconut milk	17.0	225kcal/944kJ
Coconut milk, reduced-fat	8.6	137kcal/575kJ
Coconut cream	68.8	669kcal/2760kJ

DAIRY PRODUCTS		
Cheese, hard	34.4	412kcal/1708kJ
Cheese, hard, reduced fat	15.0	261kcal/1091kJ
Cheese, cottage	3.9	98kcal/413kJ
Cheese, cream	47.4	439kcal/1807kJ
Cream, double (heavy)	48.0	449kcal/1849kJ
Cream, reduced-fat double (heavy)	24.0	243kcal/1002kJ
Cream, single (light)	19.1	198kcal/817kJ
Cream, whipping	39.3	373kcal/1539kJ
Crème fraîche	40.0	379kcal/156kJ
Crème fraîche, reduced fat	15.0	165kcal/683kJ
Fromage frais, plain	7.1	113kcal/469kJ
Fromage frais, very low-fat	0.2	58kcal/247kJ
Milk, full cream (whole)	3.9	66kcal/275kJ
Milk, semi-skimmed (low-fat)	1.5	35kcal/146kJ
Milk, skimmed	0.1	33kcal/130kJ
Yogurt, low-fat natural (plain)	0.8	56kcal/236kJ
Yogurt, Greek (US strained plain)	9.1	115kcal/477kJ

Below: Vegetables are very low in fat. Eat them raw for a filling snack, or steam them to retain maximum nutritional value.

Below: Soya products, such as tofu, soya milk and soya beans, contain isoflavones that are thought to lower cholesterol levels.

SOUPS

In China, Thailand and South-east Asian countries such as
Indonesia and Malaysia, soups are more often than not served
throughout the meal. They offer a healthy, low-fat flavoursome
choice that provides the palate with tastes and textures that
complement or contrast with main dishes. Any of these soups are
also ideal served for a light lunch or supper, so there's
something for everyone.

SPICY GREEN BEAN SOUP ★

THE POPULAR SOUP IS MADE WITH GREEN BEANS, BUT ANY SEASONAL VEGETABLES CAN BE ADDED OR SUBSTITUTED. THE RECIPE ALSO INCLUDES SHRIMP PASTE AND CHOPPED NUTS.

2 Finely grind the chopped garlic, macadamia nuts or almonds, shrimp paste and the coriander seeds to a paste using a pestle and mortar or in a food processor.

3 Heat the oil in a wok, and fry the onion until transparent. Remove with a slotted spoon. Add the nut paste to the wok and fry it for 2 minutes without allowing it to brown.

4 Add the reserved vegetable water to the wok and stir well. Add the reduced-fat coconut milk to the wok, bring to the boil and add the bay leaves. Cook the soup, uncovered, for 15–20 minutes.

SERVES EIGHT

INGREDIENTS
  225g/8oz green beans
  1.2 litres/2 pints/5 cups lightly
    salted water
  1 garlic clove, roughly chopped
  2 macadamia nuts or 4 almonds,
    finely chopped
  1cm/¹/₂ in cube shrimp paste
  10–15ml/2–3 tsp coriander seeds,
    dry fried
  15ml/1 tbsp sunflower oil
  1 onion, finely sliced
  400ml/14fl oz can reduced-fat
    coconut milk
  2 bay leaves
  225g/8oz/4 cups beansprouts
  8 thin lemon wedges
  30ml/2 tbsp lemon juice
  salt and ground black pepper

1 Trim the beans, then cut them into small pieces. Bring the lightly salted water to the boil, add the beans to the pan and cook for 3–4 minutes. Drain, reserving the cooking water. Set the beans aside.

COOK'S TIP
Dry fry the coriander seeds for about 2 minutes until the aroma is released.

5 Just before serving, reserve a few green beans, fried onions and beansprouts for garnish and stir the rest into the soup and heat through. Add the lemon wedges, lemon juice and seasoning; stir well. Pour into individual soup bowls and serve, garnished with reserved green beans, onion and beansprouts.

Energy 51kcal/212kJ; Protein 2.2g; Carbohydrate 5.2g, of which sugars 4.2g; Fat 2.5g, of which saturates 0.4g, of which polyunsaturates 1.2g; Cholesterol 3mg; Calcium 43mg; Fibre 1.2g; Sodium 84mg.

TOFU SOUP <u>WITH</u> MUSHROOMS <u>AND</u> TOMATO ★

THIS LIGHT, CLEAR BROTH IS PERFECT TO BALANCE A MEAL THAT MAY INCLUDE SOME HEAVIER MEAT OR POULTRY DISHES. THE TOFU AND MUSHROOMS ABSORB ALL THE DELICIOUS FLAVOURS.

SERVES FOUR

INGREDIENTS
   115g/4oz/scant 2 cups dried shiitake
      mushrooms, soaked in water for
      20 minutes
   5ml/1 tsp sunflower oil
   2 shallots, halved and sliced
   2 Thai chillies, seeded and sliced
   4cm/1½ in fresh root ginger, peeled
      and grated or finely chopped
   15ml/1 tbsp fish paste
   350g/12oz tofu, rinsed, drained
      and cut into bitesize cubes
   4 tomatoes, skinned, seeded and
      cut into thin strips
   salt and ground black pepper
   1 bunch coriander (cilantro),
      stalks removed, finely chopped,
      to garnish
For the stock
   1 meaty chicken carcass
   25g/1oz dried squid or shrimp,
      soaked in water for 15 minutes
   2 onions, peeled and quartered
   2 garlic cloves, crushed
   7.5cm/3in fresh root ginger,
      chopped
   15ml/1 tbsp fish paste
   6 black peppercorns
   2 star anise
   4 cloves
   1 cinnamon stick
   sea salt

1 To make the stock, put the chicken carcass in a deep pan. Drain and rinse the dried squid or shrimp. Add to the pan with the remaining stock ingredients, except the salt, and pour in 2 litres/3½ pints/8 cups water.

2 Bring to the boil, and boil for a few minutes, skim off any foam, then reduce the heat and simmer with the lid on for 1½–2 hours.

3 Remove the lid and continue simmering the stock for a further 30 minutes to reduce. Skim off any fat, season, then strain and measure out 1.5 litres/2½ pints/6¼ cups.

4 Squeeze dry the soaked shiitake mushrooms, remove the stems and slice the caps into thin strips. Heat the oil in a large pan or wok and stir in the shallots, chillies and ginger. As the fragrance begins to rise, stir in the fish paste, followed by the stock.

5 Add the tofu, mushrooms and tomatoes and bring to the boil. Reduce the heat and simmer for 5–10 minutes. Season to taste and sprinkle the finely chopped fresh coriander over the top. Serve piping hot.

Energy 100kcal/418kJ; Protein 8.8g; Carbohydrate 5.2g, of which sugars 4.5g; Fat 5g, of which saturates 0.7g, of which polyunsaturates 2.6g; Cholesterol 0mg; Calcium 480mg; Fibre 1.8g; Sodium 32mg.

OMELETTE SOUP ★

A VERY SATISFYING BUT HEALTHY SOUP THAT IS QUICK AND EASY TO PREPARE.

SERVES FOUR

INGREDIENTS
   1 egg
   5ml/1 tsp sunflower oil
   900ml/1½ pints/3¾ cups
      vegetable stock
   2 large carrots, finely diced
   4 leaves pak choi (bok choy),
      shredded
   30ml/2 tbsp soy sauce
   2.5ml/½ tsp granulated sugar
   2.5ml/½ tsp ground black pepper
   fresh coriander (cilantro) leaves,
      to garnish

VARIATION
Use Savoy cabbage instead of pak choi.
In Thailand there are about forty
different types of pak choi, including
miniature versions.

1 Put the egg in a bowl and beat lightly.
Heat the oil in a frying pan until it is
hot. Pour in the egg and swirl the pan
so that it coats the base evenly.

2 Cook over a medium heat until the
omelette has set and the underside is
golden. Slide it out of the pan and roll it
up like a pancake. Slice into 5mm/¼in
rounds and set aside for the garnish.

3 Put the stock into a large pan. Add
the carrots and pak choi and bring
to the boil. Reduce the heat and simmer
for 5 minutes, then add the soy sauce,
granulated sugar and pepper.

4 Stir well, then pour into warmed
bowls. Lay a few omelette rounds on the
surface of each portion and complete
the garnish with the coriander leaves.

Energy 52kcal/217kJ; Protein 3.4g; Carbohydrate 4.1g, of which sugars 3.8g; Fat 2.6g, of which saturates 0.6g, of which polyunsaturates 0.9g; Cholesterol 48mg; Calcium 100mg; Fibre 1.7g; Sodium 628mg.

BAMBOO SHOOT, FISH AND RICE SOUP ★

THIS IS A REFRESHING SOUP MADE WITH FRESHWATER FISH SUCH AS CARP OR CATFISH.

SERVES FOUR

INGREDIENTS
- 75g/3oz/scant ½ cup long grain rice, well rinsed
- 250ml/8fl oz/1 cup reduced-fat coconut milk
- 30ml/2 tbsp fish sauce
- 2 lemon grass stalks, trimmed and crushed
- 25g/1oz galangal, thinly sliced
- 2–3 Thai chillies
- 4 garlic cloves, crushed
- 15ml/1 tbsp palm sugar
- 1 fresh bamboo shoot, peeled, boiled in water for 10 minutes, and sliced
- 450g/1lb freshwater fish fillets, such as carp or catfish, skinned and cut into bitesize pieces
- 1 small bunch fresh basil leaves
- 1 small bunch fresh coriander (cilantro), chopped, and 1 chilli, finely sliced, to garnish
- rice or noodles, to serve

For the stock
- 450g/1lb pork ribs
- 1 onion, quartered
- 225g/8oz carrots, cut into chunks
- 25g/1oz dried squid or dried shrimp, soaked in water for 30 minutes, rinsed and drained
- 15ml/1 tbsp fish sauce
- 15ml/1 tbsp soy sauce
- 6 black peppercorns
- salt

1 To prepare the stock, put the ribs in a large pan and cover with 2.5 litres/4¼ pints/10 cups water. Bring to the boil, skim off any fat, and add the remaining stock ingredients. Cover the pan and simmer for 1 hour, then skim off any foam or fat.

2 Simmer the stock, uncovered, for a further 1–1½ hours, until it has reduced. Check the seasoning and strain the stock into another pan. There should be approximately 2 litres/3½ pints/7¾ cups of stock.

3 Bring the pan of stock to the boil. Stir in the rice and reduce the heat. Add the coconut milk, fish sauce, lemon grass, galangal, chillies, garlic and sugar. Simmer for about 10 minutes to let the flavours mingle. The rice should be just cooked, with bite to it.

4 Add the sliced bamboo shoot and the pieces of fish. Simmer for 5 minutes, until the fish is cooked. Check the seasoning and stir in the basil leaves. Ladle the soup into bowls, garnish with the chopped coriander and chilli, and serve with the rice or noodles.

Energy 269kcal/1130kJ; Protein 35.5g; Carbohydrate 23.2g, of which sugars 7.9g; Fat 3.8g, of which saturates 1.1g, of which polyunsaturates 0.9g; Cholesterol 87mg; Calcium 109mg; Fibre 2.6g; Sodium 214mg

GINGER, CHICKEN AND COCONUT SOUP ★

THIS AROMATIC AND CREAMY TASTING SOUP IS RICH WITH COCONUT MILK AND INTENSELY FLAVOURED WITH GALANGAL, LEMON GRASS AND KAFFIR LIME LEAVES.

SERVES SIX

INGREDIENTS

    4 lemon grass stalks, roots trimmed
    2 × 400ml/14fl oz cans reduced-fat
      coconut milk
    475ml/16fl oz/2 cups chicken stock
    2.5cm/1in piece galangal, peeled and
      thinly sliced
    10 black peppercorns, crushed
    10 kaffir lime leaves, torn
    300g/11oz chicken breast fillets,
      cut into thin strips
    115g/4oz/1 cup button (white)
      mushrooms
    50g/2oz/1/2 cup baby corn cobs,
      quartered lengthways
    60ml/4 tbsp lime juice
    45ml/3 tbsp fish sauce
    fresh red chillies, spring onions and
      fresh coriander (cilantro), to garnish

1 Cut off the lower 5cm/2in from each lemon grass stalk and chop it finely. Bruise the remaining pieces of stalk. Bring the coconut milk and chicken stock to the boil in a large pan. Add all the lemon grass, the galangal, peppercorns and half the lime leaves, lower the heat and simmer gently for 10 minutes. Strain into a clean pan.

2 Return the soup to the heat, then add the chicken, mushrooms and corn. Simmer for 5–7 minutes or until the chicken is cooked.

3 Stir in the lime juice and fish sauce, then add the remaining lime leaves. Serve hot, garnished with chopped chillies, spring onions and coriander.

HOT-AND-SOUR PRAWN SOUP ★

THIS IS A CLASSIC SEAFOOD SOUP, PROBABLY THE MOST POPULAR AND WELL-KNOWN SOUP FROM SOUTH-EAST ASIA. THERE ARE MANY VARIATIONS OF THIS FAMOUS DISH.

SERVES SIX

INGREDIENTS

    450g/1lb raw king prawns (jumbo
      shrimp), thawed if frozen
    1 litre/1³/4 pints/4 cups chicken
      stock or water
    3 lemon grass stalks, root trimmed
    10 kaffir lime leaves, torn in half
    225g/8oz can straw mushrooms
    45ml/3 tbsp fish sauce
    60ml/4 tbsp lime juice
    30ml/2 tbsp chopped spring onion
      (scallion)
    15ml/1 tbsp fresh coriander
      (cilantro) leaves
    4 fresh red chillies, seeded
      and thinly sliced
    salt and ground black pepper

1 Shell the prawns, putting the shells in a colander. Devein and set aside.

2 Rinse the shells under cold water to remove all grit and sand, then put in a large pan with the chicken stock or water. Bring to the boil.

3 Bruise the lemon grass stalks with a pestle or mallet and add them to the stock with half the lime leaves. Simmer gently for 5–6 minutes, until the stock is fragrant.

4 Strain the stock, return it to the clean pan and reheat. Add the drained mushrooms and the prawns, then cook until the prawns turn pink.

5 Stir in the fish sauce, lime juice, spring onion, coriander, chillies and the remaining lime leaves. Taste and adjust the seasoning. The soup should be sour, salty, spicy and hot.

Top: Energy 90kcal/383kJ; Protein 13.2g; Carbohydrate 7.4g, of which sugars 7.2g; Fat 1.1g, of which saturates 0.4g, of which polyunsaturates 0.2g; Cholesterol 35mg; Calcium 44mg; Fibre 0.3g; Sodium 807mg.
Bottom: Energy 69kcal/292kJ; Protein 14.5g; Carbohydrate 1.1g, of which sugars 1g; Fat 0.8g, of which saturates 0.1g, of which polyunsaturates 0.2g; Cholesterol 146mg; Calcium 81mg; Fibre 0.9g; Sodium 682mg.

PIQUANT PRAWN LAKSA ★

Energy 224kcal/939kJ; Protein 15.7g; Carbohydrate 33.7g, of which sugars 3.6g; Fat 2.9g, of which saturates 0.5g, of which polyunsaturates 1.4g; Cholesterol 130mg; Calcium 108mg; Fibre 0.5g; Sodium 206mg

THIS SPICY SOUP TASTES JUST AS GOOD WHEN MADE WITH ANY FLAKED COOKED FISH. IF YOU ARE SHORT OF TIME, BUY READY-MADE LAKSA PASTE, WHICH IS AVAILABLE FROM MANY ASIAN STORES.

2 To make the spicy paste, place the freshly prepared chopped lemon grass, seeded and chopped red chillies, sliced fresh root ginger, shrimp paste, chopped garlic cloves, ground turmeric and tamarind paste in a mortar and pound with a pestle to form a smooth paste. Alternatively, put the ingredients in a food processor instead of a mortar and whizz until a smooth paste is formed.

3 Heat the vegetable oil in a large pan, add the spicy paste and fry, stirring constantly, for a few moments to release all the flavours, but be careful not to let it burn.

SERVES THREE

INGREDIENTS

115g/4oz rice vermicelli or noodles
10ml/2 tsp vegetable oil
750ml/1¼ pints/3 cups fish stock
200ml/7fl oz/scant 1 cup coconut milk
30ml/2 tbsp fish sauce
½ lime
18 cooked peeled prawns (shrimp)
salt and cayenne pepper
60ml/4 tbsp fresh coriander (cilantro) sprigs, chopped, to garnish

For the spicy paste
2 lemon grass stalks, finely chopped
2 fresh red chillies, seeded and chopped
2.5cm/1in piece fresh root ginger, peeled and sliced
2.5ml/½ tsp dried shrimp paste
2 garlic cloves, chopped
2.5ml/½ tsp ground turmeric
30ml/2 tbsp tamarind paste

1 Cook the rice vermicelli or noodles in a large pan of boiling salted water according to the instructions on the packet. Tip the vermicelli or noodles into a large strainer, then rinse them under cold water until the liquid runs clear, and drain. Keep warm.

VARIATION
Replace the rice vermicelli or noodles with fresh egg noodles for a more substantial soup.

4 Add the fish stock and coconut milk and bring to the boil. Stir in the fish sauce, then simmer for 5 minutes. Season with salt and cayenne to taste, adding a squeeze of lime. Add the prawns and heat through for a few seconds.

5 Divide the noodles among three soup plates. Pour over the soup, making sure that each portion includes an equal number of prawns. Garnish with coriander and serve piping hot.

CRAB AND ASPARAGUS SOUP ★

Energy 75kcal/313kJ; Protein 6.6g; Carbohydrate 5.2g, of which sugars 2.4g; Fat 3.3g, of which saturates 0.6g, of which polyunsaturates 1.4g; Cholesterol 46mg; Calcium 49mg; Fibre 1.2g; Sodium 476mg.

ASPARAGUS COMBINED WITH CRAB MAKES A DELICIOUS LOW-FAT SOUP. SERVE THIS SOUP AS A LIGHT LUNCH OR SUPPER WITH PLAIN RICE VERMICELLI OR THIN EGG NOODLES.

SERVES SIX

INGREDIENTS
350g/12oz asparagus spears, trimmed and halved
900ml/1½ pints/3¾ cups chicken stock, preferably home-made
15ml/1 tbsp sunflower oil
6 shallots, chopped
115g/4oz crab meat, fresh or canned, chopped
15ml/1 tbsp cornflour (cornstarch), mixed to a paste with water
30ml/2 tbsp fish sauce
1 egg, lightly beaten
chopped chives, plus extra chives to garnish
salt and ground black pepper to taste

1 Cook the asparagus spears in the chicken stock for 5–6 minutes until tender. Drain, reserving the stock.

2 Heat the oil and stir-fry the shallots for 2 minutes. Add the asparagus spears, crab meat and chicken stock.

3 Bring the mixture to the boil and cook for 3 minutes, then remove the wok or pan from the heat and spoon some of the liquid into the cornflour mixture. Return this to the wok or pan and stir until the soup begins to thicken slightly.

4 Stir in the fish sauce, with salt and pepper to taste, then pour the beaten egg into the soup, stirring briskly so that the egg forms threads. Finally, stir the chopped chives into the soup and serve immediately, garnished with chives.

COOK'S TIP
If fresh asparagus isn't available, use 350g/12oz can asparagus. Drain and halve the spears.

COCONUT AND SEAFOOD SOUP ★

THE LONG LIST OF INGREDIENTS COULD MISLEAD YOU INTO THINKING THAT THIS SOUP IS COMPLICATED AND VERY TIME-CONSUMING TO PREPARE. IN FACT, IT IS EXTREMELY EASY TO MAKE.

SERVES FOUR

INGREDIENTS

750ml/1¼ pints/3 cups fish stock
5 thin slices fresh root ginger
2 lemon grass stalks, chopped
3 kaffir lime leaves, shredded
bunch garlic chives, about
  25g/1oz
small bunch fresh coriander
  (cilantro), about 15g/½oz
5ml/1 tsp sunflower oil
4 shallots, chopped
250ml/8fl oz/1 cup reduced-fat
  coconut milk
30–45ml/2–3 tbsp fish sauce
45ml/3 tbsp green curry paste
350g/12oz raw large prawns
  (shrimp), peeled and deveined
350g/12oz prepared squid
a little fresh lime juice (optional)
salt and ground black pepper
30ml/2 tbsp crisp fried shallot
  slices, to serve

1 Pour the fish stock into a large pan and add the slices of ginger, the chopped lemon grass and half the shredded kaffir lime leaves.

2 Reserve a few garlic chives for the garnish, then chop the remainder. Add half the chopped garlic chives to the pan. Strip the coriander leaves from the stalks and set the leaves aside. Add the stalks to the pan. Bring to the boil, reduce the heat, cover, then simmer for 20 minutes. Strain the stock into a bowl.

3 Rinse and dry the pan. Add the oil and shallots. Cook over a medium heat for 5–10 minutes, until the shallots are just beginning to brown.

4 Stir in the strained stock, coconut milk, the remaining kaffir lime leaves and 30ml/2 tbsp of the fish sauce. Heat over a low heat for 5–10 minutes.

5 Stir in the curry paste and prawns, then cook for 3 minutes. Add the squid and cook for a further 2 minutes. Add the lime juice, if using, and season, adding more fish sauce to taste. Stir in the remaining chives and the reserved coriander leaves. Serve in bowls and sprinkle each portion with fried shallots and whole garlic chives.

VARIATIONS
• Instead of squid, you could add 400g/14oz firm white fish, such as monkfish, cut into small pieces.
• You could also replace the squid with mussels. Steam 675g/1½lb live mussels in a tightly covered pan for 3–4 minutes, or until they have opened. Discard any that remain shut, then remove them from their shells and add to the soup.

Energy 164kcal/692kJ; Protein 29.7g; Carbohydrate 4.5g, of which sugars 3.4g; Fat 3.1g, of which saturates 0.7g, of which polyunsaturates 1.2g; Cholesterol 368mg; Calcium 137mg; Fibre 0.5g; Sodium 363mg.

PRAWN AND PORK SOUP WITH RICE STICKS ★

IN THIS LOW-FAT AND HEALTHY SOUP, THE PORK STOCK IS ENHANCED WITH THE INTENSE SWEET AND SMOKY FLAVOUR OF DRIED SQUID, AND THE MARRIAGE OF FLAVOURS WORKS BEAUTIFULLY.

SERVES FOUR

INGREDIENTS
  225g/8oz lean pork tenderloin
  225g/8oz dried rice sticks
    (vermicelli), soaked in lukewarm
    water for 20 minutes
  20 prawns (shrimp), shelled
    and deveined
  115g/4oz/½ cup beansprouts
  2 spring onions (scallions),
    finely sliced
  2 green or red Thai chillies, seeded
    and finely sliced
  1 garlic clove, finely sliced
  1 bunch each coriander (cilantro)
    and basil, stalks removed, leaves
    roughly chopped
  1 lime, cut into quarters, and
    nuoc cham, to serve
For the stock
  25g/1oz dried squid
  450g/1lb pork ribs
  1 onion, peeled and quartered
  225g/8oz carrots, peeled and cut
    into chunks
  15ml/1 tbsp fish sauce
  15ml/1 tbsp soy sauce
  6 black peppercorns
  salt

1 To make the stock, soak the dried squid in water for 30 minutes, rinse and drain. Put the ribs in a large pan and cover with approximately 2.5 litres/ 4½ pints/10 cups water. Bring to the boil, skim off any fat, and add the dried squid with the remaining stock ingredients. Cover the pan and simmer for 1 hour, then skim off any foam or fat and continue to simmer, uncovered, for a further 1½ hours.

2 Strain the stock and check the seasoning. You should have roughly 2 litres/3½ pints/8 cups.

COOK'S TIP
Nuoc cham is a popular Vietnamese dipping sauce made from chillies. If you can't find *nuoc cham*, any other sweet chilli sauce will work just as well.

3 Pour the stock into a wok or deep pan and bring to the boil. Reduce the heat, add the pork tenderloin and simmer for 25 minutes. Lift the tenderloin out of the stock, place it on a board and cut it into thin slices. Meanwhile, keep the stock simmering gently over a low heat.

4 Bring a pan of water to the boil. Drain the rice sticks and add to the water. Cook for about 5 minutes, or until tender, separating them with chopsticks if they stick together. Drain the rice sticks and divide them among four warm bowls.

5 Drop the prawns into the simmering stock for 1 minute. Lift them out with a slotted spoon and layer them with the slices of pork on top of the rice sticks. Ladle the hot stock over them and sprinkle with beansprouts, spring onions, chillies, garlic and herbs. Serve each bowl of soup with a wedge of lime to squeeze over it and *nuoc cham* to splash on top.

Energy 234kcal/981kJ; Protein 26.2g; Carbohydrate 24.8g, of which sugars 1.6g; Fat 3.3g, of which saturates 1g, of which polyunsaturates 0.6g; Cholesterol 137mg; Calcium 84mg; Fibre 1.1g; Sodium 681mg.

CRISPY WONTON SOUP ★

THE FRESHLY COOKED CRISP WONTONS ARE SUPPOSED TO SIZZLE AND "SING" IN THE HOT SOUP AS
THEY ARE TAKEN TO THE TABLE. ALTHOUGH IT CONTAINS WONTONS THIS RECIPE IS VERY LOW IN FAT.

SERVES SIX

INGREDIENTS
    2 cloud ear (wood ear) mushrooms,
      soaked for 30 minutes in warm
      water to cover
    1.2 litres/2 pints/5 cups
      home-made chicken stock
    2.5cm/1in piece fresh root ginger,
      peeled and grated
    4 spring onions (scallions), chopped
    2 rich-green inner spring greens
      (collards) leaves, finely shredded
    50g/2oz drained canned bamboo
      shoots, sliced
    25ml/1½ tbsp dark soy sauce
    2.5ml/½ tsp sesame oil
    salt and ground black pepper
For the filled wontons
    2.5ml/½ tsp sesame oil
    ½ small onion, finely chopped
    10 drained canned water
      chestnuts, finely chopped
    115g/4oz minced (ground) lean pork
    24 wonton wrappers
    1 egg white
    5ml/1 tsp sunflower oil

1 Make the filled wontons. Heat the sesame oil in a small pan. When hot, add the finely chopped onion and water chestnuts and the lean pork and cook, stirring often, until the meat is no longer pink but not overbrown. Tip the mixture into a bowl, season to taste and leave to cool.

VARIATION
For a delicious soup that is even lower in fat, replace the pork with an equivalent quantity of minced (ground) lean chicken or turkey breast fillets. Season well with freshly ground black pepper.

2 Place the wonton wrappers under a slightly dampened dish towel so that they do not dry out. Next, dampen the edges of a wonton wrapper. Place about 5ml/1 tsp of the filling in the centre of the wrapper. Gather it up like a purse and pinch together well. Fill the remaining wontons in the same way.

3 Make the soup. Drain the cloud ears, trim away any rough stems, then slice thinly. Bring the stock to the boil, add the ginger and the spring onions and simmer for 3 minutes. Add the sliced cloud ears, shredded spring greens, bamboo shoots and soy sauce. Simmer for 10 minutes, then stir in the sesame oil. Season to taste with salt and pepper, cover and keep hot.

4 Meanwhile, preheat the oven to 240°C/475°F/Gas 9. Lightly whisk the egg white with the sunflower oil and water. Brush the wontons generously with egg white and place them on a non-stick baking sheet. Bake for about 5 minutes, until browned and crisp. Ladle the soup into six warmed soup bowls and share the wontons among them. Serve immediately.

COOK'S TIP
The wontons can be sprinkled with 5ml/1 tsp toasted sesame seeds for extra flavour and crunch. To toast sesame seeds, put them in a dry frying pan and place over a medium heat until the seeds change colour. Shake the pan constantly so that the seeds brown evenly and do not burn.

Energy 132kcal/554kJ; Protein 8.4g; Carbohydrate 17g, of which sugars 3.4g; Fat 3.9g, of which saturates 0.7g, of which polyunsaturates 1.9g; Cholesterol 12mg; Calcium 140mg; Fibre 2.7g; Sodium 332mg.

HOT AND SOUR SOUP ★

ONE OF CHINA'S MOST POPULAR SOUPS, THIS IS FAMED FOR ITS CLEVER BALANCE OF FLAVOURS. THE "HOT" COMES FROM PEPPER; THE "SOUR" FROM VINEGAR. OTHER RECIPES USE CHILLIES AND LIME JUICE.

SERVES SIX

INGREDIENTS

4–6 Chinese dried mushrooms
2–3 small pieces of cloud ear (wood ear) mushrooms and a few golden needles (lily buds), optional
115g/4oz lean pork fillet, cut into fine strips
45ml/3 tbsp cornflour (cornstarch)
150ml/¼ pint/⅔ cup water
15ml/1 tbsp sunflower oil
1 small onion, finely chopped
1.5 litres/2½ pints/6¼ cups good quality beef or chicken stock, or 2 × 300g/11oz cans consommé made up to the full quantity with water
150g/5oz drained fresh firm tofu, diced
60ml/4 tbsp rice vinegar
15ml/1 tbsp light soy sauce
1 egg, beaten
salt and ground white or black pepper
2–3 spring onions (scallions), shredded, to garnish

2 Lightly dust the strips of pork fillet with some of the cornflour; mix the remaining cornflour to a smooth paste with the measured water.

3 Heat the oil in a wok or pan and fry the onion until soft. Increase the heat and fry the pork until it changes colour. Add the stock or consommé, mushrooms, soaking water, and cloud ears and golden needles, if using. Bring to the boil, then simmer for 15 minutes.

4 Discard the golden needles, lower the heat and stir in the cornflour paste to thicken. Add the tofu, vinegar, soy sauce, and salt and pepper.

5 Bring the soup to just below boiling point, then drizzle in the beaten egg by letting it drop from a balloon whisk (or to be authentic, from the fingertips) so that it forms threads in the gently simmering soup. Serve immediately, garnished with spring onion shreds.

1 Place the dried mushrooms in a bowl, with the pieces of cloud ear and the golden needles, if using. Add sufficient warm water to cover and leave to soak for about 30 minutes. Drain the mushrooms, reserving the soaking water. Cut off and discard the mushroom stems and slice the caps finely. Trim away any tough stem from the cloud ears, then chop them finely. Using kitchen string, tie the golden needles into a bundle.

Energy 102kcal/426kJ; Protein 7.7g; Carbohydrate 8g, of which sugars 0.8g; Fat 4.8g, of which saturates 1g, of which polyunsaturates 2g; Cholesterol 44mg; Calcium 140mg; Fibre 0.2g; Sodium 273mg.

BEEF NOODLE SOUP ★

Energy 391kcal/1633kJ; Protein 14.9g; Carbohydrate 70.5g, of which sugars 1.9g; Fat 4.3g, of which saturates 1.6g, of which polyunsaturates 0.3g; Cholesterol 24mg; Calcium 41mg; Fibre 1.1g; Sodium 398mg.

MADE WITH BEEF OR CHICKEN, THIS SOUP IS STREET FOOD, WORKING MEN'S FOOD AND FAMILY FOOD.
IT IS NUTRITIOUS, PARTICULARLY LOW IN FAT, AND MAKES AN INTENSELY SATISFYING MEAL.

SERVES SIX

INGREDIENTS

250g/9oz beef sirloin, trimmed
500g/1¼lb dried noodles, soaked in
  lukewarm water for 20 minutes
1 onion, halved and finely sliced
6–8 spring onions (scallions),
  cut into long pieces
2–3 red Thai chillies, seeded and
  finely sliced
115g/4oz/½ cup beansprouts
1 large bunch each fresh coriander
  (cilantro) and mint, stalks removed,
  leaves chopped
2 limes, cut in wedges, and hoisin
  sauce, fish sauce, *nuoc cham* or
  another dipping sauce to serve

For the stock

1.5kg/3lb 5oz oxtail, trimmed of fat
  and cut into thick pieces
1kg/2¼lb beef shank or brisket
2 large onions, peeled and quartered
2 carrots, peeled and cut into chunks
7.5cm/3in fresh root ginger,
  cut into chunks
6 cloves
2 cinnamon sticks
6 star anise
5ml/1 tsp black peppercorns
30ml/2 tbsp soy sauce
45–60ml/3–4 tbsp fish sauce
salt

1 To make the stock, put the oxtail into a large, deep pan and cover it with water. Bring it to the boil and blanch the meat for about 10 minutes. Drain the meat, rinsing off any scum, and clean out the pan.

2 Put the blanched oxtail back into the pan with the other stock ingredients, apart from the fish sauce and salt, and cover with about 3 litres/5¼ pints/12 cups water. Bring it to the boil, reduce the heat and simmer, covered, for 2–3 hours.

3 Remove the lid and simmer for another hour, until the stock has reduced to about 2 litres/3½ pints/ 8 cups. Skim off any fat and then strain the stock into another pan.

4 Cut the beef sirloin across the grain into thin pieces, the size of the heel of your hand. Bring the stock to the boil once more, stir in the fish sauce, season to taste, then reduce the heat and leave the stock simmering until ready to use.

5 Meanwhile, bring a pan filled with water to the boil, drain the rice sticks and add to the water. Cook for about 5 minutes or until tender – you may need to separate them with a pair of chopsticks if they look as though they are sticking together.

6 Drain the noodles and divide them equally among six wide soup bowls. Top each serving with the slices of beef, onion, spring onions, chillies and beansprouts.

7 Ladle the hot stock over the top of these ingredients, top with the fresh herbs and serve with the lime wedges to squeeze over. Pass around the hoisin sauce, fish sauce or *nuoc cham* for those who like a little sweetening, fish flavouring or extra fire.

COOK'S TIPS

• The key to this soup is a tasty, light stock flavoured with ginger, cinnamon, cloves and star anise, so it is worth cooking it slowly and leaving it to stand overnight to allow the flavours to develop.
• To enjoy this dish, use your chopsticks to lift the noodles through the layers of flavouring and slurp them up. This is the essence of Vietnam.
• *Nuoc cham* is a popular Vietnamese dipping sauce made from chillies.

APPETIZERS AND SNACKS

Flavoursome ingredients, such as garlic, ginger, coriander, spring onions, limes, lemon grass and chillies are combined to make appetizers and snacks that are both irresistible and delicious. Treat yourself and your guests to healthy dishes such as crunchy Spring Rolls with Mushrooms and Pork, chunky Fish Cakes with Cucumber Relish and succulent Soft-shell Crabs with Chilli and Salt.

POTATO, SHALLOT AND GARLIC SAMOSAS ★

MOST SAMOSAS ARE DEEP-FRIED. THESE THAI SNACKS ARE BAKED, MAKING THEM A HEALTHIER OPTION.
THEY ARE PERFECT FOR PARTIES, SINCE THE PASTRIES NEED NO LAST-MINUTE ATTENTION.

MAKES TWENTY-FIVE

INGREDIENTS
1 large potato, about 250g/
9oz, diced
15ml/1 tbsp sunflower oil
2 shallots, finely chopped
1 garlic clove, finely chopped
60ml/4 tbsp reduced-fat
coconut milk
5ml/1 tsp Thai red or green
curry paste
75g/3oz/¾ cup peas
juice of ½ lime
25 samosa wrappers or 10 x 5cm/
4 x 2in strips of filo pastry
salt and ground black pepper
oil, for brushing

1 Preheat the oven to 220°C/425°F/
Gas 7. Bring a small pan of water to the
boil, add the diced potato, cover and
cook for 10–15 minutes, until tender.
Drain and set aside.

2 Meanwhile, heat the sunflower oil in
a large frying pan and cook the shallots
and garlic over a medium heat, stirring
occasionally, for 4–5 minutes, until
softened and golden.

COOK'S TIP
Many Asian food stores sell what is
described as a samosa pad. This is a
packet, usually frozen, containing about
50 oblong pieces of samosa pastry. Filo
pastry, cut to size, can be used instead.

3 Add the drained diced potato,
coconut milk, red or green curry paste,
peas and lime juice to the frying pan.
Mash together coarsely with a wooden
spoon. Season to taste with salt and
pepper and cook over a low heat for
2–3 minutes, then remove the pan from
the heat and set aside until the mixture
has cooled a little.

4 Lay a samosa wrapper or filo strip
flat on the work surface. Brush with
a little oil, then place a generous
teaspoonful of the potato mixture in
the middle of one end. Turn one corner
diagonally over the filling to meet the
long edge.

5 Continue folding over the filling,
keeping the triangular shape as you
work down the strip. Brush with a little
more oil if necessary and place on a
baking sheet. Prepare all the other
samosas in the same way.

6 Bake for 15 minutes, or until the
pastry is golden and crisp. Leave to
cool slightly before serving.

Energy 42kcal/178kJ; Protein 1.2g; Carbohydrate 8.5g, of which sugars 0.6g; Fat 0.6g, of which saturates 0.1g, of which polyunsaturates 0.4g; Cholesterol 0mg; Calcium 14mg; Fibre 0.5g; Sodium 4mg.

GREEN CURRY PUFFS ★

SHRIMP PASTE AND GREEN CURRY SAUCE, USED JUDICIOUSLY, GIVE THESE PUFFS THEIR DISTINCTIVE, SPICY, SAVOURY FLAVOUR, AND THE ADDITION OF CHILLI STEPS UP THE HEAT.

MAKES TWENTY-FOUR

INGREDIENTS
- 24 small wonton wrappers, about 8cm/3¼in square, thawed if frozen
- 15ml/1 tbsp cornflour (cornstarch), mixed to a paste with 30ml/ 2 tbsp water
- 5ml/1 tsp sunflower oil

For the filling
- 1 small potato, about 115g/4oz, boiled and mashed
- 25g/1oz/3 tbsp cooked petits pois (baby peas)
- 25g/1oz/3 tbsp cooked corn
- few sprigs fresh coriander (cilantro), chopped
- 1 small fresh red chilli, seeded and finely chopped
- ½ lemon grass stalk, finely chopped
- 15ml/1 tbsp soy sauce
- 5ml/1 tsp shrimp paste or fish sauce
- 5ml/1 tsp Thai green curry paste

1 Combine the filling ingredients. Lay out one wonton wrapper and place a teaspoon of the filling in the centre.

2 Brush a little of the cornflour paste along two sides of the square. Fold the other two sides over to meet them, then press together to make a triangular pastry and seal in the filling. Make more pastries in the same way, thinning the paste with a little water if it becomes too thick.

3 Preheat the oven to 240°C/475°F/ Gas 9 and prepare a non-stick baking tray or line a baking tray with baking parchment. Lightly whisk the egg white with the oil and 5ml/1 tsp water.

4 Brush the pastries generously with the egg white and place on the baking sheet. Bake for about 5–8 minutes, until browned and crisp. If you intend serving the puffs hot, place them in a low oven while cooking successive batches. The puffs also taste good cold.

COOK'S TIP
Wonton wrappers dry out quickly, so keep them covered, using clear film (plastic wrap), until you are ready to use them.

Energy 32kcal/134kJ; Protein 1g; Carbohydrate 6.7g, of which sugars 0.4g; Fat 0.3g, of which saturates 0g, of which polyunsaturates 0.1g; Cholesterol 1mg; Calcium 16mg; Fibre 0.4g; Sodium 58mg.

FISH CAKES WITH CUCUMBER RELISH ★

THESE WONDERFUL SMALL FISH CAKES ARE A VERY FAMILIAR AND POPULAR APPETIZER IN THAILAND AND INCREASINGLY THROUGHOUT SOUTH-EAST ASIA. THEY ARE USUALLY SERVED WITH THAI BEER.

MAKES ABOUT TWELVE

INGREDIENTS
    5 kaffir lime leaves
    300g/11oz cod, cut into chunks
    30ml/2 tbsp red curry paste
    1 egg
    30ml/2 tbsp Thai fish sauce
    5ml/1 tsp sugar
    30ml/2 tbsp cornflour (cornstarch)
    15ml/1 tbsp chopped fresh
      coriander (cilantro)
    50g/2oz green beans, finely sliced
    spray vegetable oil, for frying
    Chinese mustard cress,
      to garnish
For the cucumber relish
    60ml/4 tbsp coconut or rice vinegar
    50g/2oz/¼ cup sugar
    1 head pickled garlic
    15ml/1 tbsp fresh root ginger
    1 cucumber, cut into matchsticks
    4 shallots, finely sliced

1 Make the cucumber relish. Bring the vinegar and sugar to the boil in a small pan with 60ml/4 tbsp water, stirring until the sugar has dissolved. Remove from the heat and cool.

2 Separate the pickled garlic into cloves. Chop these finely along with the ginger and place in a bowl. Add the cucumber and shallots, pour over the vinegar mixture and mix lightly.

3 Reserve two kaffir lime leaves for garnish and thinly slice the remainder. Put the chunks of fish, curry paste and egg in a food processor and process to a smooth paste. Transfer the mixture to a bowl and stir in the fish sauce, sugar, cornflour, sliced kaffir lime leaves, coriander and green beans. Mix well, then shape the mixture into about twelve 5mm/¼in thick cakes, measuring about 5cm/2in in diameter.

4 Spray the oil in a non-stick wok or deep-frying pan. Fry the fish cakes, a few at a time, for about 4–5 minutes until cooked and evenly brown.

5 Lift out the fish cakes and drain them on kitchen paper. Keep each batch hot while frying successive batches. Garnish with the reserved kaffir leaves and Chinese mustard cress. Serve with the cucumber relish.

Energy 54kcal/228kJ; Protein 5.4g; Carbohydrate 6.4g, of which sugars 5g; Fat 0.9g, of which saturates 0.2g, of which polyunsaturates 0.2g; Cholesterol 27mg; Calcium 12mg; Fibre 0.2g; Sodium 22mg.

SOFT-SHELL CRABS WITH CHILLI AND SALT ★★

IF FRESH SOFT-SHELL CRABS ARE UNAVAILABLE, YOU CAN BUY FROZEN ONES IN ASIAN SUPERMARKETS. ALLOW TWO SMALL CRABS PER SERVING, OR ONE IF THEY ARE LARGE.

SERVES FOUR

INGREDIENTS
8 small soft-shell crabs, thawed
   if frozen
50g/2oz/½ cup plain
   (all-purpose) flour
15ml/1 tbsp sunflower oil
2 large fresh red chillies, or
   1 green and 1 red, seeded and
   thinly sliced
4 spring onions (scallions) or a
   small bunch of garlic chives,
   chopped
coarse sea salt and ground
   black pepper
To serve
   shredded lettuce, mooli (daikon)
      and carrot
   light soy sauce

1 Pat the crabs dry with kitchen paper. Season the flour with pepper and coat the crabs lightly with the mixture.

2 Heat the oil in a shallow pan until very hot, then put in the crabs (you may need to do this in two batches). Fry for 2–3 minutes on each side, until the crabs are golden brown but still juicy in the middle. Drain the cooked crabs on kitchen paper and keep hot.

3 Add the sliced chillies and spring onions or garlic chives to the oil remaining in the pan and cook gently for about 2 minutes. Sprinkle over a generous pinch of salt, then spread the mixture on to the crabs.

4 Mix the shredded lettuce, mooli and carrot together. Arrange on plates, top each portion with two crabs and serve, with light soy sauce for dipping.

Energy 133kcal/558kJ; Protein 11.1g; Carbohydrate 10g, of which sugars 0.4g; Fat 5.7g, of which saturates 0.7g, of which polyunsaturates 2.6g; Cholesterol 36mg; Calcium 21mg; Fibre 0.5g; Sodium 211mg.

POPIAH ★

Do not be put off by the number of ingredients used in this dish. It does take a little time to get everything together but once all the preparation is completed and it is all on the table the cook can retire as guests assemble their own.

MAKES ABOUT TWENTY-FOUR PANCAKES

INGREDIENTS
  40g/1½oz/⅓ cup cornflour
    (cornstarch)
  215g/7½oz/generous 1¾ cups
    plain (all-purpose) flour
  salt
  450ml/¾ pint/scant 2 cups water
  6 eggs, beaten
  spray sunflower oil, for frying
For the cooked filling
  15ml/1 tbsp sunflower oil
  1 onion, finely chopped
  2 garlic cloves, crushed
  115g/4oz cooked lean pork, chopped
  115g/4oz crab meat or peeled
    cooked prawns (shrimp), thawed
    if frozen
  115g/4oz drained canned bamboo
    shoot, thinly sliced
  1 small yam bean, peeled and grated
    or 12 drained canned water
    chestnuts, finely chopped
  15–30ml/1–2 tbsp yellow
    salted beans
  15ml/1 tbsp light soy sauce
  ground black pepper
For the fresh fillings
  2 hard-boiled eggs, chopped
  2 Chinese sausages, steamed
    and sliced
  115g/4oz packet fried tofu, each
    piece halved
  225g/8oz/4 cups beansprouts
  115g/4oz crab meat or peeled
    cooked prawns (shrimp)
  ½ cucumber, cut into matchsticks
  small bunch of spring onions
    (scallions), finely chopped
  20 lettuce leaves, rinsed and dried
  fresh coriander (cilantro) sprigs,
    to garnish
  selection of sauces, including bottled
    chopped chillies, bottled chopped
    garlic and hoisin sauce, to serve

COOK'S TIP
Yam beans are large tubers with a mild sweet taste similar to water chestnuts.

1 Sift the flours and salt into a bowl. Add the measured water and eggs and mix to a smooth batter.

2 Spray a heavy non-stick frying pan with sunflower oil, then pour in just enough batter to cover the base.

3 As soon as it sets, flip and cook the other side. The pancakes should be quite thin. Repeat with the remaining batter to make 20–24 pancakes in all. Pile the cooked pancakes on top of each other, with a layer of baking parchment between each to prevent them sticking. Wrap in foil and keep warm in a low oven.

4 Make the cooked filling for the popiah. Heat the oil in a wok and stir-fry the onion and garlic together for 5 minutes until softened but not browned. Add the pork, crab meat or prawns, bamboo shoot and grated yam bean or water chestnuts. Stir-fry the mixture over a medium heat for 2–3 minutes.

5 Add the salted yellow beans and soy sauce to the wok, with pepper to taste. Cover and cook the beans gently for 15–20 minutes, adding a little boiling water if the mixture starts to dry out. Spoon into a serving bowl and allow to cool.

6 Meanwhile, arrange the chopped hard-boiled eggs, sliced Chinese sausages, sliced tofu, beansprouts, crab meat or prawns, cucumber matchsticks, finely chopped spring onions and lettuce leaves in piles on a large platter or in separate bowls. Spoon the bottled chopped chillies, bottled chopped garlic and hoisin into small bowls.

7 To serve, arrange the popiah on a large warm platter. Each person makes up his or her own popiah by spreading a very small amount of chopped chilli, garlic or hoisin sauce on a pancake, adding a lettuce leaf, a little of the cooked filling and a small selection of the fresh ingredients. The pancake wrapper should not be over-filled.

8 The ends can be tucked in and the pancake rolled up in typical spring roll fashion, then eaten in the hand. They also look attractive simply rolled with the filling showing. The popiah can be filled and rolled before guests arrive, in which case, garnish with sprigs of coriander. It is more fun though for everyone to fill and roll their own.

Energy 94kcal/396kJ; Protein 6.7g; Carbohydrate 10g, of which sugars 0.7g; Fat 3.4g, of which saturates 0.8g, of which polyunsaturates 0.8g; Cholesterol 88mg; Calcium 60mg; Fibre 0.6g; Sodium 109mg.

CRUNCHY SUMMER ROLLS ★

THESE DELIGHTFUL RICE PAPER ROLLS FILLED WITH CRUNCHY RAW SUMMER VEGETABLES AND
FRESH MINT AND CORIANDER ARE LIGHT AND REFRESHING, EITHER AS A SNACK OR AN APPETIZER
TO A MEAL, AND ARE ENJOYED ALL OVER CHINA AND THAILAND.

2 Work with one paper at a time. Place a lettuce leaf towards the edge nearest to you, leaving about 2.5cm/1in to fold over. Place a mixture of the vegetables on top, followed by some mint and coriander leaves.

3 Fold the edge nearest to you over the filling, tuck in the sides, and roll tightly to the edge on the far side. Place the filled roll on a plate and cover with clear film (plastic wrap), so it doesn't dry out. Repeat with the remaining rice papers and vegetables. Serve with a dipping sauce of your choice. If you are making these summer rolls ahead of time, keep them in the refrigerator under a damp dish towel, so that they remain moist.

COOK'S TIPS

• In Vietnam, these crunchy filled rolls are often served with a light peanut dipping sauce. In Cambodia, they are accompanied by a dipping sauce called *tuk trey* (also the name of the national fish sauce), which is similar to the Vietnamese dipping sauce, *nuoc cham*, except that it has chopped peanuts in it. They are, in fact, delicious with any dipping sauce.
• Rice papers can be bought in Chinese and South-east Asian markets.

VARIATION

This recipe only uses vegetables, which are cut into equal lengths, but you can also add pre-cooked shredded lean chicken, pork or prawns (shrimp) to summer rolls.

SERVES FOUR

INGREDIENTS
  12 round rice papers
  1 lettuce, leaves separated and ribs removed
  2–3 carrots, cut into julienne strips
  1 small cucumber, peeled, halved lengthways and seeded, and cut into julienne strips
  3 spring onions (scallions), trimmed and cut into julienne strips
  225g/8oz mung beansprouts
  1 bunch fresh mint leaves
  1 bunch coriander (cilantro) leaves
  dipping sauce, to serve
    (see Cook's Tips)

1 Pour some lukewarm water into a shallow dish. Soak the rice papers, 2–3 at a time, for about 5 minutes until they are pliable. Place the soaked papers on a clean dish towel and cover with a second dish towel to keep them moist.

Energy 107kcal/447kJ; Protein 3.9g; Carbohydrate 20.6g, of which sugars 4.4g; Fat 0.9g, of which saturates 0.1g, of which polyunsaturates 0.3g; Cholesterol 0mg; Calcium 62mg; Fibre 2.9g; Sodium 16mg.

SPRING ROLLS WITH MUSHROOMS AND PORK ★

ONE OF THE MOST POPULAR FOODS THROUGHOUT CHINA AND THAILAND IS THE SPRING ROLL, WHICH MAKES AN IDEAL QUICK SNACK. EVEN THOUGH THE SPRING ROLLS ARE DEEP FRIED, THE BRIEF COOKING TIME AND CAREFUL DRAINING ON KITCHEN PAPER MEANS THEY ARE VERY LOW IN FAT.

MAKES ABOUT 30

INGREDIENTS
30 dried rice wrappers
sunflower oil, for deep-frying
1 bunch fresh mint, stalks removed
For the filling
50g/2oz dried bean thread
(cellophane) noodles, soaked in
warm water for 20 minutes
25g/1oz dried cloud ear (wood ear)
mushrooms, soaked in warm water
for 15 minutes
2 eggs
30ml/2 tbsp fish sauce
2 garlic cloves, crushed
10ml/2 tsp sugar
1 onion, finely chopped
3 spring onions (scallions),
finely sliced
350g/12oz/1½ cups minced (ground)
lean pork
175g/6oz/1¾ cups cooked crab meat
or raw prawns (shrimp)
salt and ground black pepper

1 To make the filling, squeeze dry the soaked noodles and chop them into small pieces. Squeeze dry the soaked dried cloud ear mushrooms and chop them.

2 Beat the eggs in a bowl. Stir in the fish sauce, garlic and sugar. Add the onion, spring onions, noodles, mushrooms, pork and crab meat or prawns. Season well with salt and ground black pepper.

COOK'S TIP
These spring rolls are filled with rice noodles and served with fresh mint. You can substitute beansprouts for the noodles to create rolls more akin to the traditional version. Fresh mint leaves give these rolls a refreshing bite, but fresh coriander (cilantro), basil or flat leaf parsley will work just as well and give an interesting flavour. Dipped into a piquant sauce of your choice, the rolls are very moreish.

3 Have ready a damp dish towel, some clear film (plastic wrap) and a bowl of water. Dip a rice wrapper in the water and place it on the damp towel. Spoon about 15ml/1 tbsp of the spring roll filling on to the side nearest to you, just in from the edge. Fold the nearest edge over the filling, fold over the sides, tucking them in neatly, and then roll the whole wrapper into a tight cylinder. Place the roll on a plate and cover with clear film to keep it moist. Continue making spring rolls in the same way, using the remaining wrappers and filling.

4 Heat the sunflower oil in a wok or heavy pan for deep-frying. Make sure it is hot enough by dropping in a small piece of bread; it should foam and sizzle. Cook the spring rolls in batches, turning them in the oil so that they become golden all over. Drain them on kitchen paper and serve immediately with mint leaves to wrap around them and a dipping sauce of your choice.

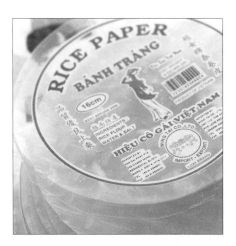

Energy 55kcal/232kJ; Protein 4.5g; Carbohydrate 7g, of which sugars 0.4g; Fat 0.9g, of which saturates 0.3g, of which polyunsaturates 0.1g; Cholesterol 31mg; Calcium 10mg; Fibre 0.1g; Sodium 24mg.

PRAWN TOASTS WITH SESAME SEEDS ★

THIS HEALTHY VERSION OF THE EVER-POPULAR APPETIZER HAS LOST NONE OF ITS CLASSIC CRUNCH AND TASTE. SERVE IT AS A SNACK, TOO. IT IS GREAT FOR GETTING A PARTY OFF TO A GOOD START.

2 Meanwhile, put the prawns in a food processor with the water chestnuts, egg white, sesame oil and salt. Process the mixture, using the pulse facility if you have it, until a coarse purée is formed.

3 Scrape the mixture into a bowl, stir in the chopped spring onions and sherry and set aside for 10 minutes at room temperature to allow the flavours to mix.

4 Remove the toast from the oven and raise the temperature to 200°C/400°F/ Gas 6. Spread the prawn mixture on the toast, sprinkle with the sesame seeds and bake for 12 minutes. Garnish the prawn toasts with spring onion and serve hot or warm.

COOK'S TIP
To toast sesame seeds, put them in a dry frying pan and place over a medium heat until the seeds change colour. Shake the pan constantly so the seeds brown evenly and do not burn.

SERVES FOUR TO SIX

INGREDIENTS
  6 slices medium-cut white bread,
    crusts removed
  225g/8oz raw tiger prawns (jumbo
    shrimp), peeled and deveined
  50g/2oz/⅓ cup drained,
    canned water chestnuts
  1 egg white
  5ml/1 tsp sesame oil
  2.5ml/½ tsp salt
  2 spring onions (scallions), chopped
  10ml/2 tsp dry sherry
  15ml/1 tbsp sesame seeds, toasted
    (see Cook's Tip)
  shredded spring onion (scallion),
    to garnish

1 Preheat the oven to 120°C/250°F/ Gas ½. Using a sharp knife, cut each slice of bread into four triangles. Spread out the triangles on to a large baking sheet and bake for 25 minutes or until crisp and golden.

Energy 120kcal/506kJ; Protein 10.1g; Carbohydrate 13.8g, of which sugars 1g; Fat 2.8g, of which saturates 0.3g; Cholesterol 73mg; Calcium 80mg; Fibre 0.8g; Sodium 223mg.

PORK PÂTÉ IN A BANANA LEAF ★★

THIS PÂTÉ IS STEAMED IN BANANA LEAVES AND HAS A SLIGHTLY SPRINGY TEXTURE AND DELICATE FLAVOUR. SMEAR IT ON A FRESHLY BAKED BAGUETTE FOR A REAL TREAT.

SERVES SIX

INGREDIENTS
  45ml/3 tbsp fish sauce
  15ml/1 tbsp vegetable or sesame oil
  15ml/1 tbsp sugar
  10ml/2 tsp five-spice powder
  2 shallots, peeled and finely
    chopped
  2 garlic cloves, crushed
  675g/1½lb/3 cups minced
    (ground) pork
  25g/1oz/¼ cup potato starch
  7.5ml/1½ tsp baking powder
  1 banana leaf, trimmed into a strip
    25cm/10in wide
  vegetable oil, for brushing
  salt and ground black pepper
  a baguette or green salad leaves,
    to serve

1 In a bowl, beat the fish sauce and oil with the sugar and five-spice powder. Once the sugar has dissolved, stir in the shallots and garlic. Add the minced pork and seasoning, and knead well until thoroughly combined. Cover and chill for 2–3 hours.

2 Knead the mixture again, thumping it down into the bowl to remove any air. Add the potato starch and baking powder and knead until smooth and pasty. Mould the pork mixture into a fat sausage, about 18cm/7in long, and place it on an oiled dish.

COOK'S TIP
You can find banana leaves in African, Caribbean and Asian markets. To prepare them, trim the leaves to fit the steamer, using a pair of scissors, making sure that there is enough to fold over the pâté. If you cannot find banana leaves, you can use large spring green (collard) leaves, or several Savoy cabbage leaves instead.

VARIATION
This pâté can also be added to noodles, soups and stir-fried dishes, in which it is complemented by fresh herbs and spices.

3 Lay the banana leaf on a flat surface, brush it with a little vegetable oil, and place the pork sausage across it. Lift up the edge of the banana leaf nearest to you and fold it over the sausage mixture, tuck in the sides, and roll it up into a firm, tight bundle. Secure the bundle with a piece of string, so that it doesn't unravel during the cooking process.

4 Fill a wok one-third full with water. Balance a bamboo steamer, with its lid on, above the level of the water. Bring to the boil, lift the lid and place the banana leaf bundle on the rack, being careful not to burn yourself. Re-cover and steam for 45 minutes. Leave the pâté to cool in the leaf, open it up and cut it into slices. Serve with a baguette or green salad leaves.

Energy 187kcal/783kJ; Protein 24.5g; Carbohydrate 6.7g, of which sugars 3.2g; Fat 6.9g, of which saturates 1.9g, of which polyunsaturates 2.1g; Cholesterol 71mg; Calcium 13mg; Fibre 0.2g; Sodium 79mg.

PORK ᴼᴺ LEMON GRASS STICKS ★

THIS SIMPLE RECIPE MAKES A SUBSTANTIAL SNACK, AND THE LEMON GRASS STICKS NOT ONLY ADD A SUBTLE FLAVOUR BUT ALSO MAKE A GOOD TALKING POINT AT THE DINNER TABLE.

SERVES FOUR

INGREDIENTS

    300g/11oz minced (ground)
      lean pork
    4 garlic cloves, crushed
    4 fresh coriander (cilantro) roots,
      finely chopped
    2.5ml/½ tsp granulated sugar
    15ml/1 tbsp soy sauce
    salt and ground black pepper
    8 x 10cm/4in lengths of lemon
      grass stalk
    sweet chilli sauce, to serve

VARIATION

Slimmer versions of these pork sticks are perfect for parties. The mixture will be enough for 12 lemon grass sticks if you use it sparingly.

1 Place the minced pork, crushed garlic, chopped coriander root, sugar and soy sauce in a large bowl. Season with salt and pepper to taste and mix well.

2 Divide into eight portions and mould each one into a ball. It may help to dampen your hands before shaping the mixture to prevent it from sticking.

3 Stick a length of lemon grass halfway into each ball, then press the meat mixture around the lemon grass to make a shape like a chicken leg.

4 Cook the pork sticks under a hot grill (broiler) for 3–4 minutes on each side, until golden and cooked through. Serve with the chilli sauce for dipping.

Energy 111kcal/467kJ; Protein 17.5g; Carbohydrate 3.3g, of which sugars 1.4g; Fat 3.2g, of which saturates 1.1g, of which polyunsaturates 0.6g; Cholesterol 47mg; Calcium 29mg; Fibre 1g; Sodium 323mg.

LAMB SATÉ ★

THESE TASTY LAMB SKEWERS ARE TRADITIONALLY SERVED WITH DAINTY DIAMOND-SHAPED PIECES OF COMPRESSED RICE, WHICH ARE SURPRISINGLY SIMPLE TO MAKE. OFFER THE REMAINING SAUCE FOR DIPPING.

MAKES THIRTY SKEWERS

INGREDIENTS

  1kg/2¼lb leg of lamb, boned
  3 garlic cloves, crushed
  15–30ml/1–2 tbsp chilli sambal or
    5–10ml/1–2 tsp chilli powder
  90ml/6 tbsp dark soy sauce
  juice of 1 lemon
  salt and ground black pepper
  spray sunflower oil, for spraying
For the chilli sauce
  6 garlic cloves, crushed
  15ml/1 tbsp chilli sambal or
    2–3 fresh chillies, seeded and
    ground to a paste
  90ml/6 tbsp dark soy sauce
  25ml/1½ tbsp lemon juice
  30ml/2 tbsp boiling water
To serve
  thinly sliced onion
  cucumber wedges (optional)
  compressed-rice shapes (see
    Cook's Tip)

1 Cut the lamb into neat 1cm/½in cubes. Remove any pieces of gristle, and trim off any excess fat. Spread out the lamb cubes in a single layer in a shallow bowl.

2 Put the garlic, chilli sambal or chilli powder, soy sauce and lemon juice in a mortar. Add salt and pepper and grind to a paste. Alternatively, process the mixture using a food processor. Pour over the lamb and mix to coat. Cover and leave in a cool place for at least 1 hour. Soak wooden or bamboo skewers in water to prevent them from scorching during cooking.

3 Prepare the chilli sauce. Put the crushed garlic into a bowl. Add the chilli sambal or fresh chillies, soy sauce, lemon juice and boiling water. Stir well. Preheat the grill.

4 Thread the meat on to the skewers. Spray the skewered meat with oil and grill, turning often. Brush the saté with a little of the sauce and serve hot, with onion, cucumber wedges, if using, rice shapes and the sauce.

COOK'S TIP
Compressed rice shapes are easy to make. Cook two 115g/4oz packets of boil-in-the-bag rice in a large pan of salted, boiling water and simmer for 1¼ hours until the cooked rice fills each bag like a plump cushion. The bags must be covered with water throughout. When cool, cut each rice slab horizontally in half, then into diamond shapes using a sharp, wetted knife.

Energy 33kcal/139kJ; Protein 3.5g; Carbohydrate 0.6g, of which sugars 0.3g; Fat 1.9g, of which saturates 0.9g, of which polyunsaturates 0.1g; Cholesterol 13mg; Calcium 2mg; Fibre 0.1g; Sodium 86mg.

LEMON GRASS SNAILS ★

THE LIVE SNAILS SOLD IN SOUTH-EAST ASIAN MARKETS ARE USUALLY DESTINED FOR THIS POPULAR DELICACY. SERVED STRAIGHT FROM THE BAMBOO STEAMER, THESE LEMON GRASS-INFUSED MORSELS ARE SERVED AS AN APPETIZER, OR AS A SPECIAL SNACK, WITH A DIPPING SAUCE OF YOUR CHOICE.

SERVES FOUR

INGREDIENTS
- 12 fresh snails in their shells
- 115g/4oz lean minced (ground) pork, passed through the mincer twice
- 2 lemon grass stalks, trimmed and finely chopped or ground (reserve the outer leaves)
- 1 spring onion (scallions), finely chopped
- 15g/½oz fresh root ginger, peeled and finely grated
- 1 red Thai chilli, seeded and finely chopped
- 5ml/1 tsp sesame oil
- sea salt and ground black pepper

2 Chop the snails finely and put them in a bowl. Add the minced pork, lemon grass, spring onions, ginger, chilli and oil. Season with salt and pepper and mix all the ingredients together.

4 Using your fingers, stuff each shell with the snail and pork mixture, gently pushing it between the lemon grass ends to the back of the shell so that it fills the shell completely.

1 Pull the snails out of their shells and place them in a colander. Rinse the snails thoroughly in plenty of cold water and pat dry with kitchen paper. Rinse the shells and leave to drain.

3 Select the best of the lemon grass leaves and tear each one into thin ribbons, roughly 7.5cm/3in long. Bend each ribbon in half and put it inside a snail shell, so that the ends are poking out. The idea is that each diner pulls the ends of the lemon grass ribbon to gently prize the steamed morsel out of its shell.

COOK'S TIP
Freshwater snails in their shells are available in South-east Asian markets, and some supermarkets and delicatessens. The idea of eating snails may have come from the French, who colonized Vietnam and Cambodia in the 19th and 20th centuries, but the method of cooking them in Vietnam is very different. Snails are plucked live from the water, straight into the bamboo steamer. If you ask for snails in a Vietnamese restaurant, they are likely to be cooked this way.

5 Fill a wok or large pan a third of the way up with water and bring it to the boil. Arrange the snail shells, open side up, in a steamer that fits the wok or pan.

6 Place the lid on the steamer and steam for about 10 minutes, until the mixture is cooked. Serve hot with any strong-flavoured dipping sauce of your choice if you wish, such as sweet chilli sauce, or soy sauce spiked with chopped chillies.

Energy 85kcal/357kJ; Protein 12g; Carbohydrate 0.4g, of which sugars 0.4g; Fat 4g, of which saturates 1.2g, of which polyunsaturates 0.9g; Cholesterol 36mg; Calcium 29mg; Fibre 0.7g; Sodium 38mg.

FISH AND SHELLFISH

Fish and shellfish are extremely popular throughout China, Thailand and South-east Asia. They can be steamed, stir-fried, baked or grilled with local spices and herbs, or served in curries and sauces. Serving a fish whole, rather than cutting it into portions, has great appeal; try spicy Hot and Fragrant Trout, or for a really impressive dish, treat your guests to fragrant Stir-fried Scallops and Prawns, or a traditional Chinese Steamboat.

SPICY PAN-SEARED TUNA WITH CUCUMBER, GARLIC AND GINGER ★★

THIS POPULAR DISH, WHICH CAN BE FOUND ALL OVER SOUTH-EAST ASIA IN RESTAURANTS OR AT FOOD STALLS, IS MADE WITH MANY TYPES OF THICK-FLESHED FISH. TUNA IS PARTICULARLY SUITABLE BECAUSE IT IS DELICIOUS PAN-SEARED AND SERVED A LITTLE RARE.

SERVES FOUR

INGREDIENTS
  1 small cucumber
  10ml/2 tsp sesame oil
  2 garlic cloves, crushed
  4 tuna steaks
For the dressing
  4cm/1½in fresh root ginger, peeled
    and roughly chopped
  1 garlic clove, roughly chopped
  2 green Thai chillies, seeded and
    roughly chopped
  45ml/3 tbsp raw cane sugar
  45ml/3 tbsp fish sauce
  juice of 1 lime
  60ml/4 tbsp water

1 To make the dressing, grind the ginger, garlic and chillies to a pulp with the sugar, using a mortar and pestle. Stir in the fish sauce, lime juice and water, and mix well. Leave the dressing to stand for 15 minutes.

2 Cut the cucumber in half lengthways and remove the seeds. Cut the flesh into long, thin strips. Toss the cucumber in the dressing and leave to soak for at least 15 minutes.

3 Wipe a heavy pan with the oil and rub the garlic around it. Heat the pan and add the tuna steaks. Sear for a few minutes on both sides, so that the outside is slightly charred but the inside is still rare. Lift the steaks on to a warm serving dish. Using tongs or chopsticks, lift the cucumber strips out of the dressing and arrange them around the steaks. Drizzle the dressing over the tuna, and serve immediately.

Energy 228kcal/959kJ; Protein 36.2g; Carbohydrate 1.5g, of which sugars 1.4g; Fat 8.6g, of which saturates 2g, of which polyunsaturates 3.1g; Cholesterol 42mg; Calcium 55mg; Fibre 1g; Sodium 76mg.

CHARCOAL-GRILLED FISH <u>WITH</u> MUNG BEANSPROUTS <u>AND</u> HERBS ★

IN THIS DISH, A WHOLE FISH IS GRILLED OVER CHARCOAL. IT IS THEN SERVED WITH SALAD LEAVES, HERBS, CHOPPED PEANUTS, AND A STRONG-FLAVOURED SAUCE. CHUNKS OF THE COOKED FISH ARE WRAPPED IN THE LEAVES AND DIPPED IN THE SAUCE.

SERVES FOUR

INGREDIENTS

  1 good-sized fish, such as trout,
    snakehead, barb or carp, gutted
    and rinsed, head removed,
    if you like
  225g/8oz mung beansprouts
  1 bunch each fresh basil, coriander
    (cilantro) and mint, stalks removed,
    leaves chopped
  1 lettuce, broken into leaves
  15ml/1 tbsp roasted unsalted
    peanuts, finely chopped
  steamed rice, to serve
For the sauce
  3 garlic cloves, chopped
  2 red Thai chillies, seeded
    and chopped
  25g/1oz fresh root ginger, peeled
    and chopped
  15ml/1 tbsp palm sugar
  45ml/3 tbsp fish sauce
  juice of 1 lime
  juice of 1 coconut

1 First prepare the sauce. Using a mortar and pestle, grind the garlic, chillies and ginger with the sugar to form a paste. Add the *tuk trey*, lime juice and coconut juice and bind well. Pour the sauce into a serving bowl.

2 Prepare the barbecue. Place the fish over the charcoal and grill it for 2–3 minutes each side, until cooked right through. Alternatively, use a conventional grill (broiler).

3 Lay out the beansprouts, herbs and lettuce leaves on a large plate and place the peanuts in a bowl. Put everything on the table, including the cooked fish, sauce and rice. Using chopsticks, if you like, lift up the charred skin and tear off pieces of fish. Place each piece on a lettuce leaf, sprinkle with beansprouts, herbs and peanuts, wrap it up and dip it into the sauce.

Energy 143kcal/604kJ; Protein 18.9g; Carbohydrate 9.1g, of which sugars 6.2g; Fat 3.7g, of which saturates 0.8g, of which polyunsaturates 1.2g; Cholesterol 64mg; Calcium 84mg; Fibre 2.5g; Sodium 69mg.

HOT AND FRAGRANT TROUT ★

THIS WICKEDLY HOT SPICE PASTE COULD BE USED AS A MARINADE FOR ANY FISH OR MEAT. THE SPICY PASTE ALSO MAKES A WONDERFUL SPICY DIP FOR GRILLED LAMB OR PORK.

SERVES FOUR

INGREDIENTS
2 large fresh green chillies, seeded and coarsely chopped
5 shallots, peeled
5 garlic cloves, peeled
30ml/2 tbsp fresh lime juice
30ml/2 tbsp Thai fish sauce
15ml/1 tbsp palm sugar or light muscovado (brown) sugar
4 kaffir lime leaves, rolled into cylinders and thinly sliced
2 trout or similar firm-fleshed fish, about 350g/12oz each, cleaned
fresh garlic chives, to garnish
boiled rice, to serve

1 Wrap the chillies, shallots and garlic in a foil package. Place under a hot grill (broiler) for 10 minutes, until softened.

2 When the package is cool enough to handle, tip the contents into a mortar or food processor and pound with a pestle or process to a paste.

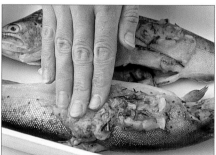

3 Add the lime juice, fish sauce, sugar and lime leaves and mix well. With a teaspoon, stuff this paste inside the fish. Smear a little on the skin too. Grill (broil) the fish for about 5 minutes on each side, until just cooked through. Lift the fish on to a platter, garnish with garlic chives and serve with rice.

Energy 117kcal/490kJ; Protein 14.8g; Carbohydrate 7.9g, of which sugars 6.7g; Fat 3.1g, of which saturates 0.7g, of which polyunsaturates 1g; Cholesterol 59mg; Calcium 36mg; Fibre 0.7g; Sodium 57mg.

THAI MARINATED SEA TROUT ★

SEA TROUT HAS A SUPERB TEXTURE AND A FLAVOUR LIKE THAT OF WILD SALMON. IT IS BEST SERVED WITH STRONG BUT COMPLEMENTARY FLAVOURS, SUCH AS CHILLIES AND LIME.

SERVES SIX

INGREDIENTS
6 sea trout cutlets, each about
  115g/4oz
2 garlic cloves, chopped
1 fresh long red chilli, seeded
  and chopped
45ml/3 tbsp chopped Thai basil
15ml/1 tbsp granulated sugar
3 limes
400ml/14fl oz/1⅔ cups reduced-fat
  coconut milk
spray sunflower oil
15ml/1 tbsp fish sauce

1 Place the sea trout cutlets side by side in a shallow dish. Using a pestle, pound the chopped garlic and chilli in a large mortar to break both up roughly. Add 30ml/2 tbsp of the chopped Thai basil with the sugar and continue to pound the mixture until it forms a rough paste.

2 Grate the rind from 1 lime and squeeze it. Mix the rind and juice into the chilli paste, with the reduced-fat coconut milk. Pour the mixture over the cutlets. Cover and chill for about 1 hour. Cut the remaining limes into wedges.

3 Spray a hinged wire fish basket or grill rack with oil. Remove the cutlets from the marinade and place them in the fish basket or directly on the grill rack. Cook the fish for 4 minutes on each side, trying not to move them. They may stick to the grill rack if not seared first.

4 Strain the remaining marinade into a pan, reserving the contents of the sieve. Bring the marinade to the boil, then simmer gently for 5 minutes, stirring. Stir in the contents of the sieve and continue to simmer for 1 minute more. Add the Thai fish sauce and the remaining Thai basil.

5 Lift each fish cutlet on to a plate, pour over the sauce and serve with the lime wedges.

COOK'S TIP
Sea trout is best cooked when the barbecue is cool to medium hot, and the coals have a medium to thick coating of ash. Take care when cooking any fish in a marinade, as the residue can cause flare-ups if it drips on to the coals.

VARIATION
If you prefer you could substitute wild or farmed salmon for the sea trout. Be careful not to overcook it.

Energy 158kcal/666kJ; Protein 23.1g; Carbohydrate 6.1g, of which sugars 6.1g; Fat 4.7g, of which saturates 0.1g, of which polyunsaturates 0g; Cholesterol 0mg; Calcium 48mg; Fibre 0.4g; Sodium 142mg.

GRIDDLED SQUID AND TOMATOES ★

THIS IS A LOVELY DISH — SWEET, CHARRED SQUID SERVED IN A TANGY DRESSING MADE WITH TAMARIND, LIME AND FISH SAUCE. IT IS BEST MADE WITH BABY SQUID BECAUSE THEY ARE TENDER AND SWEET. THE TOMATOES AND HERBS ADD WONDERFUL FRESH FLAVOURS.

2 Heat a ridged griddle, spray the pan with a little oil, and griddle the tomatoes until lightly charred on both sides. Transfer them to a board, chop into bitesize chunks, and place in a bowl.

3 Clean the griddle, then heat it up again and spray with a little more oil. Griddle the squid for 2–3 minutes each side, pressing them down with a spatula, until nicely browned. Transfer to the bowl with the tomatoes, add the herbs and the dressing and toss well. Serve immediately.

COOK'S TIPS
• To prepare squid yourself, get a firm hold of the head and pull it from the body. Reach down inside the body sac and then pull out and discard the transparent backbone, as well as any stringy parts. Rinse the body sac inside and out and pat dry. Cut the tentacles off above the eyes and add to the pile of squid you're going to cook. Discard everything else.
• Griddled scallops and prawns (shrimp) are also delicious in this tangy dressing.

SERVES FOUR

INGREDIENTS
    spray sunflower oil, for greasing
    2 large tomatoes, skinned, halved
      and seeded
    500g/1¼lb fresh baby squid
    1 bunch each fresh basil, coriander
      (cilantro) and mint, stalks removed,
      leaves chopped
For the dressing
    15ml/1 tbsp tamarind paste
    juice of half a lime
    30ml/2 tbsp fish sauce
    15ml/1 tbsp raw cane sugar
    1 garlic clove, crushed
    2 shallots, halved and finely sliced
    2 Serrano chillies, seeded and sliced

1 Put all the ingredients for the dressing into a large bowl and stir until well mixed. Set aside.

VARIATION
You can steam the squid for 10–15 minutes for a delicious low-fat meal.

Energy 153kcal/651kJ; Protein 20.4g; Carbohydrate 13.2g, of which sugars 11.3g; Fat 2.6g, of which saturates 0.6g, of which polyunsaturates 0.9g; Cholesterol 281mg; Calcium 54mg; Fibre 1.6g; Sodium 149mg.

STIR-FRIED PRAWNS <u>WITH</u> TAMARIND ★

THE SOUR, TANGY FLAVOUR THAT IS CHARACTERISTIC OF MANY THAI DISHES COMES FROM TAMARIND. FRESH TAMARIND PODS FROM THE TAMARIND TREE CAN SOMETIMES BE BOUGHT, BUT PREPARING THEM FOR COOKING IS A LABORIOUS PROCESS. IT IS MUCH EASIER TO USE A BLOCK OF TAMARIND PASTE.

SERVES FOUR TO SIX

INGREDIENTS
  6 dried red chillies
  15ml/1 tbsp sunflower oil
  30ml/2 tbsp chopped onion
  30ml/2 tbsp palm sugar or light
    muscovado (brown) sugar
  30ml/2 tbsp water
  15ml/1 tbsp fish sauce
  90ml/6 tbsp tamarind juice, made
    by mixing tamarind paste with
    warm water
  450g/1lb raw prawns
    (shrimp), peeled
  15ml/1 tbsp fried chopped garlic
  30ml/2 tbsp fried sliced shallots
  2 spring onions (scallions), chopped,
    to garnish

1 Heat a wok or large frying pan, but do not add any oil at this stage. Add the dried chillies and dry-fry them by pressing them against the surface of the wok or pan with a spatula, turning them occasionally. Do not let them burn. Set them aside to cool slightly.

2 Add the oil to the wok or pan and reheat. Add the chopped onion and cook over a medium heat, stirring occasionally, for 2–3 minutes, until softened and golden brown.

3 Add the sugar, water, fish sauce, dry-fried red chillies and the tamarind juice, stirring constantly until the sugar has dissolved. Bring to the boil, then lower the heat slightly.

4 Add the prawns, garlic and shallots. Toss over the heat for 3–4 minutes, until the prawns are cooked. Garnish with the spring onions and serve.

COOK'S TIP
Leave a few prawns in their shells for a garnish, if you like.

Energy 100kcal/422kJ; Protein 13.6g; Carbohydrate 6.6g, of which sugars 6g; Fat 2.3g, of which saturates 0.3g, of which polyunsaturates 1.3g; Cholesterol 146mg; Calcium 65mg; Fibre 0.3g; Sodium 321mg.

STIR-FRIED SCALLOPS AND PRAWNS ★

THIS COMBINATION OF FRESH SEAFOOD AND LIGHTLY COOKED VEGETABLES PRODUCES A DISH THAT IS HIGH IN FLAVOUR AND LOW IN FAT. SERVE IT WITH AROMATIC STEAMED RICE OR FINE RICE NOODLES.

SERVES FOUR

INGREDIENTS
15ml/1 tbsp sunflower oil
500g/1¼lb raw tiger prawns
  (shrimp), peeled
1 star anise
225g/8oz scallops, halved if large
2.5cm/1in piece fresh root ginger,
  peeled and grated
2 garlic cloves, thinly sliced
1 red (bell) pepper, seeded and cut
  into thin strips
115g/4oz/1¾ cups shiitake or button
  (white) mushrooms, thinly sliced
juice of 1 lemon
5ml/1 tsp cornflour (cornstarch)
30ml/2 tbsp light soy sauce
chopped fresh chives,
  to garnish
salt and ground black pepper

1 Heat the oil in a wok until very hot. Put in the prawns and star anise and stir-fry over a high heat for 2 minutes. Add the scallops, ginger and garlic and stir-fry for 1 minute more, by which time the prawns should have turned pink and the scallops should be opaque. Season with a little salt and plenty of pepper and then remove from the wok using a slotted spoon. Discard the star anise.

2 Add the red pepper and mushrooms to the wok and stir-fry for 1–2 minutes.

3 Make a cornflour paste by combining the cornflour with 30ml/2 tbsp cold water. Stir until smooth.

4 Pour the lemon juice, cornflour paste and soy sauce into the wok, bring to the boil and bubble for 1–2 minutes, stirring all the time, until the sauce is smooth and slightly thickened.

VARIATIONS
Other types of shellfish can be used in this dish. Try it with thinly sliced rings of squid, or use mussels or clams. You could even substitute bitesize chunks of firm white fish, such as monkfish, cod or haddock, for the scallops. These can be added to the dish in step 1, as with the scallops.

Energy 212kcal/892kJ; Protein 36.2g; Carbohydrate 6.6g, of which sugars 3.3g; Fat 4.6g, of which saturates 0.8g, of which polyunsaturates 2.3g; Cholesterol 270mg; Calcium 122mg; Fibre 1g; Sodium 877mg.

SALT AND PEPPER PRAWNS ★

IN THIS CLASSIC CHINESE DISH, THESE SUCCULENT SHELLFISH BEG TO BE EATEN SIZZLINGLY HOT WITH THE FINGERS, SO PROVIDE FINGER BOWLS OR HOT CLOTHS FOR YOUR GUESTS.

SERVES FOUR

INGREDIENTS
15–18 large raw prawns (shrimp),
   in the shell, about 450g/1lb
15ml/1 tbsp sunflower oil
3 shallots or 1 small onion,
   very finely chopped
2 garlic cloves, crushed
1cm/$\frac{1}{2}$in piece fresh root
   ginger, peeled and very
   finely grated
1–2 fresh red chillies, seeded and
   finely sliced
2.5ml/$\frac{1}{2}$ tsp sugar or
   to taste
3–4 spring onions (scallions),
   shredded, to garnish
For the fried salt
10ml/2 tsp salt
5ml/1 tsp Sichuan peppercorns

1 Make the fried salt by dry frying the salt and peppercorns in a heavy frying pan over medium heat until the peppercorns begin to release their aroma. Leave the mixture until cool, then tip it into a mortar and crush it with a pestle.

COOK'S TIP
"Fried salt" is also known as "Cantonese salt" or simply "salt and pepper mix". It is widely used as a table condiment or as a dip for deep fried or roasted food, but can also be an ingredient in a recipe, as here. Black or white peppercorns can be substituted for the Sichuan peppercorns. For the best flavour it really is best made when required.

2 Carefully remove the heads and legs from the raw prawns and discard. Leave the body shells and the tails in place. Pat dry with sheets of kitchen paper.

3 Heat the oil in a shallow pan until very hot. Fry the prawns for 2–3 minutes each side until cooked through, then lift them out and drain thoroughly on kitchen paper.

4 Reheat the oil in the frying pan. Add the fried salt, together with the shallots or onion, garlic, ginger, chillies and sugar. Toss together for 1 minute, then add the prawns and toss them over the heat for 1 minute more until they are coated and the shells are impregnated with the seasonings. Serve immediately, garnished with the spring onions.

Energy 122kcal/514kJ; Protein 20.1g; Carbohydrate 2.7g, of which sugars 2.4g; Fat 3.5g, of which saturates 0.5g, of which polyunsaturates 1.9g; Cholesterol 219mg; Calcium 97mg; Fibre 0.3g; Sodium 1197mg.

THAI PRAWN SALAD WITH GARLIC DRESSING AND FRIZZLED SHALLOTS ★

IN THIS INTENSELY FLAVOURED SALAD, SWEET PRAWNS AND MANGO ARE PARTNERED WITH A SWEET-SOUR GARLIC DRESSING HEIGHTENED WITH THE HOT TASTE OF CHILLI. THE CRISP FRIZZLED SHALLOTS ARE A TRADITIONAL ADDITION TO THAI SALADS.

SERVES SIX

INGREDIENTS

675g/1½lb medium raw prawns
(shrimp), peeled and deveined,
with tails intact
finely shredded rind of 1 lime
½ fresh red chilli, seeded and
finely chopped
15ml/1 tbsp olive oil, plus extra
for spraying
1 ripe but firm mango
2 carrots, cut into long thin shreds
10cm/4in piece cucumber, sliced
1 small red onion, halved and
thinly sliced
a few fresh mint sprigs
a few fresh coriander (cilantro) sprigs
15ml/1 tbsp roasted peanuts,
coarsely chopped
4 large shallots, thinly sliced and
fried until crisp in 5ml/1 tsp
sunflower oil
salt and ground black pepper
For the dressing
1 large garlic clove, chopped
10–15ml/2–3 tsp caster
(superfine) sugar
juice of 2 limes
15–30ml/1–2 tbsp Thai fish sauce
1 fresh red chilli, seeded and
finely chopped
5–10ml/1–2 tsp light rice vinegar

1 Place the prawns in a glass dish with the lime rind, chilli, oil and seasoning. Toss to mix and leave to marinate at room temperature for 30–40 minutes.

2 Make the dressing. Place the garlic in a mortar with 10ml/2 tsp of the caster sugar. Pound with a pestle until smooth, then work in about three-quarters of the lime juice, followed by 15ml/1 tbsp of the Thai fish sauce.

3 Transfer the dressing to a jug (pitcher). Stir in half the chopped red chilli. Taste the dressing and add more sugar, lime juice and/or fish sauce, if you think they are necessary, and stir in light rice vinegar to taste.

4 Peel and stone (pit) the mango. The best way to do this is to cut either side of the large central stone (pit), as close to it as possible, with a sharp knife. Cut the flesh into very fine strips and cut off any flesh still adhering to the stone.

5 Place the strips of mango in a bowl and add the carrots, cucumber slices and red onion. Pour over about half the dressing and toss thoroughly. Arrange the salad on four to six individual serving plates or in bowls.

6 Heat a ridged, cast-iron griddle pan or heavy frying pan until very hot. Spray with a little oil, then sear the marinated prawns for 2–3 minutes on each side, until they turn pink and are patched with brown on the outside. Arrange the prawns on the salads.

7 Sprinkle the remaining dressing over the salads and garnish with the mint and coriander sprigs. Sprinkle over the remaining chilli with the peanuts and crisp-fried shallots. Serve immediately.

COOK'S TIP
To devein the prawns (shrimp), make a shallow cut down the back of each prawn, using a small, sharp knife. Using the tip of the knife, lift out the thin, black vein, then rinse the prawn thoroughly under cold, running water, drain it and pat it dry with kitchen paper.

Energy 156kcal/656kJ; Protein 20.9g; Carbohydrate 8.9g, of which sugars 8.4g; Fat 4.3g, of which saturates 0.7g, of which polyunsaturates 1g; Cholesterol 219mg; Calcium 102mg; Fibre 1.4g; Sodium 397mg.

SAMBAL GORENG WITH PRAWNS ★

THIS IS AN IMMENSELY USEFUL AND ADAPTABLE SAUCE. HERE IT IS COMBINED WITH PRAWNS AND GREEN PEPPER, BUT YOU COULD ADD FINE STRIPS OF FRESHLY COOKED CALF'S LIVER, CHICKEN LIVERS, TOMATOES, GREEN BEANS OR HARD-BOILED EGGS.

SERVES SIX

INGREDIENTS
  350g/12oz peeled cooked
    prawns (shrimp)
  1 green (bell) pepper, seeded
    and sliced
  60ml/4 tbsp tamarind juice
  pinch of sugar
  45ml/3 tbsp reduced-fat
    coconut milk
  boiled rice, to serve
  lime rind and red onion, to garnish
For the sambal goreng
  2.5cm/1in cube shrimp paste
  2 onions, roughly chopped
  2 garlic cloves, roughly chopped
  2.5cm/1in piece fresh galangal,
    peeled and sliced
  10ml/2 tsp chilli sambal
  1.5ml/¼ tsp salt
  15ml/1 tbsp sunflower oil
  45ml/3 tbsp tomato purée (paste)
  600ml/1 pint/2½ cups water

1 Make the sambal goreng. Grind the shrimp paste with the onions and garlic using a mortar and pestle. Alternatively put in a food processor and process to a paste. Add the galangal, chilli sambal and salt. Process or pound to a fine paste.

COOK'S TIP
Store the remaining sauce in the refrigerator for up to 3 days or freeze it for up to 3 months.

2 Heat the oil in a wok or frying pan and fry the paste for 1–2 minutes, without browning, until the mixture gives off a rich aroma. Stir in the tomato purée and the stock or water and cook for 10 minutes. Ladle half the sauce into a bowl and leave to cool. This leftover sauce can be used in another recipe (see Cook's Tip).

3 Add the prawns and green pepper to the remaining sauce. Cook over a medium heat for 3–4 minutes, then stir in the tamarind juice, sugar and coconut milk. Spoon into warmed serving bowls and garnish with strips of lime rind and sliced red onion. Serve immediately with boiled rice.

VARIATIONS
• To make tomato sambal goreng, add 450g/1lb peeled coarsely chopped tomatoes to the sauce mixture, before stirring in the stock or water.
• To make egg sambal goreng, add three or four chopped hard-boiled eggs, and two peeled chopped tomatoes to the sauce.

Energy 86kcal/359kJ; Protein 11.6g; Carbohydrate 4.6g, of which sugars 4.1g; Fat 2.4g, of which saturates 0.3g, of which polyunsaturates 1.3g; Cholesterol 118mg; Calcium 67mg; Fibre 0.9g; Sodium 175mg.

STIR-FRIED LONG BEANS <u>WITH</u> PRAWNS ★★

POPULAR THROUGHOUT SOUTH-EAST ASIA, LONG BEANS — LIKE MANY OTHER VEGETABLES — ARE OFTEN STIR-FRIED WITH GARLIC. THIS TRADITIONAL RECIPE IS MADE WITH PRAWNS, GALANGAL AND LIMES WORKS VERY WELL SERVED WITH RICE OR NOODLES.

SERVES FOUR

INGREDIENTS
    30ml/2 tbsp sunflower oil
    2 garlic cloves, finely chopped
    25g/1oz galangal, finely
      shredded
    450g/1lb fresh prawns (shrimp),
      shelled and deveined
    1 onion, halved and finely
      sliced
    450g/1lb long beans, trimmed
      and cut into 7.5cm/3in lengths
    120ml/4fl oz/½ cup soy sauce
For the marinade
    30ml/2 tbsp fish sauce
    juice of 2 limes
    10ml/2 tsp sugar
    2 garlic cloves, crushed
    1 lemon grass stalk, trimmed
      and finely sliced

1 To make the marinade, beat the fish sauce and lime juice in a bowl with the sugar, until it has dissolved. Stir in the garlic and lemon grass. Toss in the prawns, cover, and chill for 1–2 hours.

2 Heat half the oil in a wok or heavy pan. Stir in the chopped garlic and galangal. Just as they begin to colour, toss in the marinated prawns. Stir-fry for a minute or until the prawns turn pink. Lift the prawns out on to a plate, reserving as much of the oil, garlic and galangal as you can.

3 Add the remaining oil to the wok. Add the onion and stir-fry until slightly caramelized. Stir in the beans, then pour in the soy sauce. Cook for a further 2–3 minutes, until the beans are tender. Add the prawns and stir-fry for a minute until heated through. Serve immediately.

Energy 187kcal/782kJ; Protein 22.6g; Carbohydrate 9.3g, of which sugars 7.9g; Fat 6.9g, of which saturates 0.9g, of which polyunsaturates 4g; Cholesterol 219mg; Calcium 156mg; Fibre 3.2g; Sodium 485mg.

STIR-FRIED NOODLES <u>IN</u> SEAFOOD SAUCE ★

THE ADDITION OF EXTRA SPECIAL INGREDIENTS SUCH AS CRAB AND ASPARAGUS IN THIS DISH CAN MAKE A SIMPLE STIR-FRY A REAL TREAT THAT IS STILL VIRTUALLY FAT FREE.

SERVES EIGHT

INGREDIENTS
225g/8oz fresh or dried Chinese
  egg noodles
8 spring onions (scallions), cleaned
  and trimmed
8 asparagus spears, plus extra
  steamed asparagus spears, to
  serve (optional)
15ml/1 tbsp sunflower oil
5cm/2in piece fresh root ginger,
  peeled and cut into very fine
  matchsticks
3 garlic cloves, chopped
60ml/4 tbsp oyster sauce
450g/1lb cooked crab meat (all
  white, or two-thirds white and
  one-third brown)
30ml/2 tbsp rice wine
  vinegar
15–30ml/1–2 tbsp light
  soy sauce

1 Put the noodles in a large pan or wok, cover with lightly salted boiling water, place a lid on top and simmer for 3–4 minutes, or for the time suggested on the packet. Drain and set aside.

2 Cut off the green spring onion tops and slice them thinly. Set aside. Cut the white parts into 2cm/¾in lengths and quarter them lengthways. Cut the asparagus spears on the diagonal into 2cm/¾in pieces.

3 Heat the oil in a pan or wok until very hot, then add the ginger, garlic and white spring onion batons. Stir-fry over a high heat for 1 minute. Add the oyster sauce, crab meat, rice wine vinegar and soy sauce to taste. Stir-fry for about 2 minutes, until the crab and sauce are hot. Add the noodles and toss until heated through. At the last moment, toss in the spring onion tops and serve with a few extra asparagus spears, if you like.

Energy 179kcal/756kJ; Protein 14.1g; Carbohydrate 22.9g, of which sugars 3.1g; Fat 4.1g, of which saturates 0.9g, of which polyunsaturates 1.2g; Cholesterol 49mg; Calcium 82mg; Fibre 1.1g; Sodium 617mg.

CHINESE STEAMBOAT ★★

THIS CLASSIC DISH IS VERY POPULAR THROUGHOUT CHINA, AND EVERY REGION HAS THEIR OWN VERSION OF THIS HOT POT. IT IS TRADITIONALLY EATEN DURING THE WINTER MONTHS.

SERVES EIGHT

INGREDIENTS

8 Chinese dried mushrooms, soaked
  for 30 minutes in warm water
1.5 litres/2½ pints/6¼ cups well-
  flavoured chicken stock
10ml/2 tsp rice wine or
  medium-dry sherry
5ml/1 tsp sesame oil
115g/4oz each lean pork and rump
  (round) steak, thinly sliced
1 chicken breast fillet, thickly sliced
225g/8oz raw prawns
  (shrimp), peeled
450g/1lb white fish fillets, skinned
  and cubed
200g/7oz fish balls (from Asian
  food stores)
115g/4oz fried tofu, each
  piece halved
leafy green vegetables, such as
  lettuce, Chinese leaves (Chinese
  cabbage), spinach and watercress,
  cut into 15cm/6in lengths
225g/8oz rice vermicelli
8 eggs
selection of sauces, including soy
  sauce with sesame seeds; soy sauce
  with crushed ginger; chilli sauce;
  plum sauce and hot mustard
½ bunch spring onions
  (scallions), chopped
salt and ground white pepper

1 Drain the mushrooms, reserving the soaking liquid. Cut off and discard the stems; slice the caps finely.

2 Pour the stock into a large pan, with the rice wine or sherry, sesame oil and reserved mushroom liquid. Bring the mixture to the boil, then season with salt and white pepper. Reduce the heat and simmer gently while you prepare the remaining ingredients.

VARIATION
Replace the egg in step 5 with long strips of finely cut omelette for an equally delicious result.

3 Put the meat, fish, tofu, green vegetables and mushrooms in bowls on the table. Soak the vermicelli in hot water for about 5 minutes, drain and place in eight soup bowls on a small table. Crack an egg for each diner in a small bowl; place on a side table. Put the sauces in bowls beside each diner.

4 Add the chopped spring onions to the pan of stock, bring it to a full boil and fuel the steamboat. Pour the stock into the moat and seat your guests at once. Each guest lowers a few chosen morsels into the boiling stock, using chopsticks or fondue forks, leaves them for a minute or two, then removes them with a small wire mesh ladle, a fondue fork or pair of chopsticks.

5 When all the meat, fish, tofu and vegetables have been cooked, the stock will be concentrated and wonderfully enriched. Add a little boiling water if necessary. Bring the soup bowls containing the soaked noodles to the table, pour in the hot soup and slide a whole egg into each, stirring until it cooks and forms threads.

Energy 243kcal/1020kJ; Protein 35g; Carbohydrate 4.1g, of which sugars 0.8g; Fat 9.7g, of which saturates 2.6g, of which polyunsaturates 1.6g; Cholesterol 299mg; Calcium 168mg; Fibre 0.4g; Sodium 304mg.

STEAMED MUSSELS WITH CHILLI AND GINGER ★

IN THIS SIMPLE DISH, THE MUSSELS ARE STEAMED OPEN IN A HERB-INFUSED STOCK RATHER THAN IN WHITE WINE. LEMON GRASS AND CHILLI FLAVOUR THE DISH INSTEAD OF WINE AND PARSLEY.

SERVES FOUR

INGREDIENTS
600ml/1 pint/2½ cups chicken stock
1 Thai chilli, seeded and chopped
2 shallots, finely chopped
3 lemon grass stalks,
    finely chopped
1 bunch ginger or basil leaves
1kg/2¼lb fresh mussels, cleaned
    and bearded
salt and ground black pepper

COOK'S TIP
Aromatic ginger leaves are hard to find outside Asia. If you can't find them, basil or coriander (cilantro) will work well.

1 Pour the chicken stock into a deep pan. Add the chopped chilli, shallots, lemon grass and most of the ginger or basil leaves, retaining a few leaves for the garnish. Bring to the boil. Cover and simmer for 10–15 minutes, then season to taste.

2 Discard any mussels that remain open when tapped, then add the remaining mussels to the stock. Stir well, cover and cook for 2 minutes, or until the mussels have opened. Discard any that remain closed. Ladle the mussels and cooking liquid into individual bowls.

Energy 75kcal/318kJ; Protein 13.6g; Carbohydrate 1.5g, of which sugars 1.1g; Fat 1.7g, of which saturates 0.3g, of which polyunsaturates 0.5g; Cholesterol 30mg; Calcium 176mg; Fibre 0.8g; Sodium 162mg.

MUSSELS AND CLAMS WITH LEMON GRASS ★

*LEMON GRASS HAS AN INCOMPARABLE AROMATIC FLAVOUR AND IS WIDELY USED WITH ALL KINDS OF
SEAFOOD IN THAILAND AS THE FLAVOURS MARRY SO PERFECTLY.*

SERVES SIX

INGREDIENTS
    900g/2lb fresh mussels
    225g/8oz baby clams
    120ml/4fl oz/½ cup dry white wine
    1 bunch spring onions
        (scallions), chopped
    1 lemon grass stalk, chopped
    3 kaffir lime leaves, chopped
    10ml/2 tsp Thai green curry paste
    120ml/4fl oz/½ cup reduced-fat
        coconut milk
    30ml/2 tbsp chopped fresh
        coriander (cilantro)
    salt and ground black pepper
    garlic chives, to garnish

1 Clean the mussels by pulling off the
beards, scrubbing the shells well and
scraping off any barnacles with the
blade of a knife. Scrub the clams.
Discard any mussels or clams that are
damaged or broken or which do not
close immediately when tapped sharply.

2 Put the wine in a large pan with the
spring onions, lemon grass and lime
leaves. Stir in the curry paste. Simmer
until the wine has almost evaporated.

COOK'S TIPS
• In these days of marine pollution, it is
unwise to gather fresh shellfish yourself.
Those available from fish stores have
either been farmed or have undergone a
purging process to clean them.
• Depending on where you live, you may
have difficulty obtaining clams. If so, use
a few extra mussels instead.

3 Add the mussels and clams to the
pan and increase the heat to high.
Cover tightly and steam the shellfish
for 5–6 minutes, until they open.

4 Using a slotted spoon, transfer the
mussels and clams to a heated serving
bowl, cover and keep hot. Discard any
shellfish that remain closed. Strain the
cooking liquid into a clean pan through
a sieve lined with muslin (cheesecloth)
and simmer briefly to reduce to about
250ml/8fl oz/1 cup.

5 Stir the coconut milk and chopped
coriander into the sauce and season
with salt and pepper to taste. Heat
through. Pour the sauce over the
mussels and clams, garnish with the
garlic chives and serve immediately.

Energy 73kcal/309kJ; Protein 10.5g; Carbohydrate 2.1g, of which sugars 1.8g; Fat 1.2g, of which saturates 0.2g, of which polyunsaturates 0.4g; Cholesterol 26mg; Calcium 129mg; Fibre 0.7g; Sodium 271mg.

CHICKEN, DUCK, PORK AND BEEF

Poultry and meat both star in an astonishing variety of Asian recipes — they can be stir-fried with ginger or chillies, roasted with spices, grilled, stewed or curried. This chapter contains a selection of the best dishes that China, Thailand and South-east Asia have to offer, from classic curries such as Green Beef Curry with Thai Aubergines to traditional meat dishes such as Cha Shao, and Chicken Satay with Peanut Sauce.

CHICKEN SATAY <u>WITH</u> PEANUT SAUCE ★★

THESE MINIATURE KEBABS ARE POPULAR ALL OVER SOUTH-EAST ASIA. THE PEANUT DIPPING
SAUCE IS A PERFECT PARTNER FOR THE MARINATED CHICKEN.

SERVES FOUR

INGREDIENTS
  4 skinless, chicken breast fillets
For the marinade
  2 garlic cloves, crushed
  2.5cm/1in piece fresh root ginger,
    finely grated
  10ml/2 tsp Thai fish sauce
  30ml/2 tbsp light soy sauce
  15ml/1 tbsp clear honey
For the satay sauce
  45ml/3 tbsp crunchy peanut butter
  1/2 fresh red chilli, seeded and
    finely chopped
  juice of 1/2 lime
  30ml/2 tbsp reduced-fat
    coconut milk
  salt

1 First, make the satay sauce. Put all the ingredients in a food processor or blender. Process until smooth, then check the seasoning and add more salt or lime juice if necessary. Spoon the sauce into a bowl, cover with clear film (plastic wrap) and set aside.

2 Using a sharp knife, slice each chicken breast into four long strips. Put all the marinade ingredients in a large bowl and mix well, then add the chicken strips and toss together until thoroughly coated. Cover and leave for at least 30 minutes in the refrigerator to marinate. Meanwhile, soak 16 wooden satay sticks or kebab skewers in water, to prevent them from burning during cooking.

3 Preheat the grill (broiler) to high or prepare the barbecue. Drain the satay sticks or skewers. Drain the chicken strips. Thread one strip on to each satay stick or skewer. Grill (broil) for 3 minutes on each side, or until the chicken is golden brown and cooked through. Serve immediately with the satay sauce.

Energy 236kcal/992kJ; Protein 38.8g; Carbohydrate 3.4g, of which sugars 2.6g; Fat 7.5g, of which saturates 1.9g, of which polyunsaturates 2.2g; Cholesterol 105mg; Calcium 15mg; Fibre 0.6g; Sodium 672mg.

FRAGRANT GRILLED CHICKEN ★

IF YOU HAVE TIME, PREPARE THE CHICKEN IN ADVANCE AND LEAVE IT TO MARINATE IN THE REFRIGERATOR FOR SEVERAL HOURS — OR EVEN OVERNIGHT — UNTIL READY TO COOK.

SERVES FOUR

INGREDIENTS
    450g/1lb chicken breast fillets,
      with the skin on
    15ml/1 tbsp sesame oil
    2 garlic cloves, crushed
    2 coriander (cilantro) roots,
      finely chopped
    2 small fresh red chillies, seeded
      and finely chopped
    30ml/2 tbsp Thai fish sauce
    5ml/1 tsp sugar
    cooked rice, to serve
    lime wedges, to garnish
For the sauce
    90ml/6 tbsp rice vinegar
    60ml/4 tbsp sugar
    2.5ml/½ tsp salt
    2 garlic cloves, crushed
    1 small fresh red chilli, seeded and
      finely chopped
    115g/4oz/4 cups fresh coriander
      (cilantro), finely chopped

1 Lay the chicken breast fillets between two sheets of clear film (plastic wrap), baking parchment or foil and beat with the side of a rolling pin or the flat side of a meat tenderizer until the meat is about half its original thickness. Place in a large, shallow dish or bowl.

2 Mix together the sesame oil, garlic, coriander roots, red chillies, fish sauce and sugar in a jug (pitcher), stirring until the sugar has dissolved. Pour the mixture over the chicken and turn to coat. Cover with clear film and set aside to marinate in a cool place for at least 20 minutes. Meanwhile, make the sauce.

3 Heat the vinegar in a small pan, add the sugar and stir until dissolved. Add the salt and stir until the mixture begins to thicken. Add the remaining sauce ingredients, stir well, then spoon the sauce into a serving bowl.

4 Preheat the grill (broiler) and cook the chicken for 5 minutes. Turn and baste with the marinade, then cook for 5 minutes more, or until cooked through and golden. Serve with rice and the sauce, garnished with lime wedges.

Energy 221kcal/934kJ; Protein 28.3g; Carbohydrate 17.8g, of which sugars 17.7g; Fat 4.5g, of which saturates 0.8g, of which polyunsaturates 1.4g; Cholesterol 79mg; Calcium 97mg; Fibre 2.1g; Sodium 82mg.

CHICKEN <u>WITH</u> LEMON SAUCE ★

SUCCULENT CHICKEN WITH A REFRESHING LEMONY SAUCE AND JUST A HINT OF LIME IS A SURE
WINNER AS A FAMILY MEAL THAT IS QUICK AND EASY TO PREPARE.

2 Mix together the egg white and cornflour. Add the mixture to the chicken and turn the chicken with tongs until thoroughly coated. Heat the sunflower oil in a non-stick frying pan or wok and fry the chicken fillets for about 15 minutes until they are golden brown on both sides.

3 Meanwhile, make the sauce. Combine all the ingredients in a small pan. Add 1.5ml/¼ tsp salt. Bring to the boil over a low heat, stirring constantly until the sauce is smooth and has thickened.

SERVES FOUR

INGREDIENTS
    4 small skinless chicken breast fillets
    5ml/1 tsp sesame oil
    15ml/1 tbsp dry sherry
    1 egg white, lightly beaten
    30ml/2 tbsp cornflour (cornstarch)
    15ml/1 tbsp sunflower oil
    salt and ground white pepper
    chopped coriander (cilantro) leaves
      and spring onions (scallions) and
      lemon wedges, to garnish
For the sauce
    45ml/3 tbsp fresh lemon juice
    30ml/2 tbsp sweetened lime juice
    45ml/3 tbsp caster (superfine) sugar
    10ml/2 tsp cornflour (cornstarch)
    90ml/6 tbsp cold water

1 Arrange the chicken in a single layer in a bowl. Mix the sesame oil with the sherry and add 2.5ml/½ tsp salt and 1.5ml/¼ tsp pepper. Pour over the chicken, cover and marinate for 15 minutes.

VARIATIONS
Turkey fillets can be substituted for chicken in this recipe. Any white fish can also be used in this dish.

4 Cut the chicken into pieces and place on a warm serving plate. Pour the sauce over, garnish with the coriander leaves, spring onions and lemon wedges.

Energy 235kcal/995kJ; Protein 30.9g; Carbohydrate 23.3g, of which sugars 14.1g; Fat 2.2g, of which saturates 0.5g, of which polyunsaturates 0.6g; Cholesterol 88mg; Calcium 15mg; Fibre 0g; Sodium 97mg.

BARBECUE CHICKEN ★

CHICKEN COOKED ON A BARBECUE IS SERVED ALMOST EVERYWHERE IN THAILAND, FROM ROADSIDE STALLS TO SPORTS STADIA. THIS IS THE PERFECT DISH FOR A SUMMER PARTY.

SERVES FOUR TO SIX

INGREDIENTS
1 chicken, about 1.5kg/3–3½lb,
    cut into 8–10 pieces
lime wedges and fresh red chillies,
    to garnish
For the marinade
2 lemon grass stalks, roots trimmed
2.5cm/1in piece fresh root ginger,
    peeled and thinly sliced
6 garlic cloves, coarsely chopped
4 shallots, coarsely chopped
½ bunch coriander (cilantro)
    roots, chopped
15ml/1 tbsp palm sugar or light
    muscovado (brown) sugar
120ml/4fl oz/½ cup reduced-fat
    coconut milk
30ml/2 tbsp Thai fish sauce
30ml/2 tbsp light soy sauce

1 Make the marinade. Cut off the lower 5cm/2in of the lemon grass stalks and chop them coarsely. Put into a food processor with the ginger, garlic, shallots, coriander, sugar, coconut milk and sauces and process until smooth.

2 Place the chicken pieces in a dish, pour over the marinade and stir to mix well. Cover the dish and leave in a cool place to marinate for at least 4 hours, or leave it in the refrigerator overnight.

3 Prepare the barbecue or preheat the oven to 200°C/400°F/Gas 6. Drain the chicken, reserving the marinade. If you are cooking in the oven, arrange the chicken pieces in a single layer on a rack set over a roasting pan.

4 Cook the chicken on the barbecue over moderately hot coals or on medium heat for a gas barbecue, or bake in the oven for 20–30 minutes. Turn the pieces and brush with the reserved marinade once or twice during cooking.

5 As soon as the chicken pieces are golden brown and cooked through, transfer them to a serving platter, garnish with the lime wedges and red chillies and serve immediately.

COOK'S TIPS
• Coriander roots are more intensely flavoured than the leaves, but the herb is not always available with the roots intact. One answer is to grow your own, but if this is impractical, use the bottom portion of the stem as a substitute.
• Coconut milk is available in cans or cartons from Asian food stores and most supermarkets. Reduced-fat versions contain less than half the fat.

Energy 145kcal/610kJ; Protein 28.5g; Carbohydrate 2.3g, of which sugars 2g; Fat 2.4g, of which saturates 0.7g, of which polyunsaturates 0.5g; Cholesterol 108mg; Calcium 14mg; Fibre 0.1g; Sodium 458mg.

SOUTHERN CHICKEN CURRY ★★

A MILD COCONUT CURRY FLAVOURED WITH TURMERIC, CORIANDER AND CUMIN SEEDS THAT DEMONSTRATES THE INFLUENCE OF MALAYSIAN COOKING ON THAI CUISINE.

SERVES SIX

INGREDIENTS
    30ml/2 tbsp sunflower oil
    1 large garlic clove, crushed
    1 chicken, weighing about 1.5kg/
        3–3½lb, chopped into
        12 large pieces
    400ml/14fl oz/1⅔ cups reduced-fat
        coconut milk
    250ml/8fl oz/1 cup chicken stock
    30ml/2 tbsp Thai fish sauce
    30ml/2 tbsp sugar
    juice of 2 limes
To garnish
    2 small fresh red chillies, seeded and
        finely chopped
    1 bunch spring onions (scallions),
        thinly sliced
For the curry paste
    5ml/1 tsp dried chilli flakes
    2.5ml/½ tsp salt
    5cm/2in piece fresh turmeric or
        5ml/1 tsp ground turmeric
    2.5ml/½ tsp coriander seeds
    2.5ml/½ tsp cumin seeds
    5ml/1 tsp dried shrimp paste

1 First make the curry paste. Put all the ingredients in a mortar, food processor or spice grinder and pound, process or grind to a smooth paste.

2 Heat the oil in a large wok or frying pan and cook the garlic until golden. Add the chopped chicken and cook until golden. Remove the chicken from the heat and set aside.

3 Reheat the oil in the wok or frying pan. Add the curry paste and then half the coconut milk. Cook for a few minutes until fragrant.

4 Return the chicken to the wok or pan, add the stock, mixing well, then add the remaining coconut milk, the fish sauce, sugar and lime juice. Stir well and bring to the boil, then lower the heat and simmer for 15 minutes.

VARIATION
For a delicious curry that is even lower in fat, remove the skin before cooking the chicken in step 2.

5 Turn the curry into six warm serving bowls and sprinkle with the chopped fresh chillies and spring onions to garnish. Serve immediately.

COOK'S TIP
Use a large sharp knife or a Chinese cleaver to chop the chicken into pieces. Wash the board, knife and your hands thoroughly afterwards in hot, soapy water as chicken is notorious for harbouring harmful micro-organisms and bacteria.

Energy 222kcal/935kJ; Protein 29g; Carbohydrate 9.8g, of which sugars 9.5g; Fat 7.7g, of which saturates 1.7g, of which polyunsaturates 3.2g; Cholesterol 144mg; Calcium 50mg; Fibre 0.4g; Sodium 231mg.

YELLOW CHICKEN CURRY ★

THE PAIRING OF SLIGHTLY SWEET COCONUT MILK AND FRUIT WITH SAVOURY CHICKEN AND SPICES IS AT ONCE A COMFORTING, REFRESHING AND EXOTIC COMBINATION.

SERVES FOUR

INGREDIENTS
   300ml/½ pint/1¼ cups
     chicken stock
   30ml/2 tbsp thick tamarind juice,
     made by mixing tamarind paste with
     warm water
   15ml/1 tbsp granulated sugar
   200ml/7fl oz/scant 1 cup reduced-fat
     coconut milk
   1 green papaya, peeled, seeded and
     thinly sliced
   250g/9oz skinless chicken breast
     fillets, diced
   juice of 1 lime
   lime slices, to garnish
For the curry paste
   1 fresh red chilli, seeded and
     coarsely chopped
   4 garlic cloves, coarsely chopped
   3 shallots, coarsely chopped
   2 lemon grass stalks, sliced
   5cm/2in piece fresh turmeric,
     coarsely chopped, or 5ml/1 tsp
     ground turmeric
   5ml/1 tsp shrimp paste
   5ml/1 tsp salt

1 Make the yellow curry paste. Put the red chilli, garlic, shallots, lemon grass and turmeric in a mortar or food processor. Add the shrimp paste and salt. Pound or process to a paste, adding a little water if necessary.

COOK'S TIP
Fresh turmeric resembles root ginger in appearance and is a member of the same family. When preparing it, wear gloves to protect your hands from staining.

2 Pour the stock into a wok or medium pan and bring it to the boil. Stir in the curry paste. Bring back to the boil and add the tamarind juice, sugar and coconut milk. Add the papaya and chicken and cook over a medium to high heat for about 15 minutes, stirring frequently, until the chicken is cooked.

3 Stir in the lime juice, transfer to a warm dish and serve immediately, garnished with lime slices.

Energy 146kcal/619kJ; Protein 16.4g; Carbohydrate 18.6g, of which sugars 18g; Fat 1.2g, of which saturates 0.3g, of which polyunsaturates 0.2g; Cholesterol 44mg; Calcium 77mg; Fibre 3.5g; Sodium 103mg.

FRAGRANT RICE <u>WITH</u> CHICKEN ★

THIS REFRESHING DISH CAN BE SERVED AS IT IS, OR AS PART OF A MEAL THAT MIGHT INCLUDE FISH OR CHICKEN, EITHER GRILLED OR ROASTED WHOLE, AND ACCOMPANIED BY STEAMED GREENS.

2 Put the rice in a heavy pan and stir in the stock. When the rice settles, check that the stock sits roughly 2.5cm/1in above the rice; if not, top it up. Bring the liquid to the boil, cover the pan and cook for about 25 minutes, or until all the water has been absorbed.

3 Remove the pan from the heat and, using a fork, add the shredded chicken, shallots and most of the mint. Cover the pan again and leave the flavours to mingle for 10 minutes. Tip the rice into bowls, or on to a serving dish, garnish with the remaining mint and the spring onions, and serve.

SERVES FOUR

INGREDIENTS
   350g/12oz/1¾ cups long grain rice,
      rinsed and drained
   2–3 shallots, halved and finely sliced
   1 bunch of fresh mint, stalks
      removed, leaves finely shredded
   2 spring onions (scallions), finely
      sliced, to garnish
For the stock
   2 meaty chicken legs
   1 onion, peeled and quartered
   4cm/1½in fresh root ginger, peeled
      and coarsely chopped
   15ml/1 tbsp fish sauce
   3 black peppercorns
   1 bunch of fresh mint
   sea salt

1 To make the stock, put the chicken legs into a deep pan. Add all the other ingredients, except the salt, and pour in 1 litre/1¾ pints/4 cups water. Bring the water to the boil, skim off any foam, then reduce the heat and simmer gently with the lid on for 1 hour. Remove the lid, increase the heat and simmer for a further 30 minutes to reduce the stock. Skim off any fat, strain the stock and season with salt. Measure 750ml/1¼ pints/3 cups stock. Remove the chicken meat from the bone and shred.

VARIATIONS
Any meat or fish can be added to this basic recipe. Try strips of stir-fried pork, slices of Chinese sausage or a handful of prawns (shrimp). Simply toss into the rice along with the shredded chicken.

Energy 426kcal/1784kJ; Protein 25.6g; Carbohydrate 72.9g, of which sugars 1.8g; Fat 3.1g, of which saturates 0.7g, of which polyunsaturates 0.6g; Cholesterol 92mg; Calcium 53mg; Fibre 0.5g; Sodium 82mg.

CHICKEN WITH CHILLIES AND LEMON GRASS ★

THERE ARE VARIATIONS OF THIS DISH, USING PORK OR SEAFOOD, THROUGHOUT SOUTH-EAST ASIA SO, FOR A SMOOTH INTRODUCTION TO ASIAN COOKING, THIS IS A GOOD PLACE TO START.

SERVES FOUR

INGREDIENTS
  15ml/1 tbsp sugar
  15ml/1 tbsp sunflower oil
  2 garlic cloves, finely chopped
  2–3 green or red Thai chillies,
    seeded and finely chopped
  2 lemon grass stalks, finely sliced
  1 onion, finely sliced
  350g/12oz skinless chicken breast
    fillets, cut into bitesize strips
  30ml/2 tbsp soy sauce
  15ml/1 tbsp fish sauce
  1 bunch fresh coriander (cilantro),
    stalks removed, leaves chopped
  salt and ground black pepper
  dipping sauce to serve

2 Heat a large wok or heavy pan and add the sunflower oil. Stir in the chopped garlic, chillies and lemon grass, and stir-fry until they become fragrant and golden. Add the onion and stir-fry for 1 minute, then add the chicken strips.

3 When the chicken is cooked through, add the soy sauce, fish sauce and caramel sauce. Stir to mix and heat through, then season with a little salt and pepper. Toss the coriander into the chicken and serve with a dipping sauce of your liking.

1 To make a caramel sauce, put the sugar into a pan with 5ml/1 tsp water. Heat gently until the sugar has dissolved and turned golden. Set aside.

Energy 142kcal/598kJ; Protein 21.6g; Carbohydrate 5.5g, of which sugars 5.1g; Fat 3.9g, of which saturates 0.6g, of which polyunsaturates 1.9g; Cholesterol 61mg; Calcium 35mg; Fibre 0.8g; Sodium 57mg.

CRISPY ROAST DUCK ★★

HERE IS A VERSION OF THE POPULAR CHINESE DISH, PEKING DUCK. THE SUCCULENT, CRISPY BIRD IS USUALLY ENJOYED IN ONE COURSE. YOU CAN SERVE IT WITH PANCAKES OR STEAMED RICE.

2 Preheat the oven to 220°C/425°F/Gas 7. Stuff the ginger, garlic, lemon grass and spring onions into the duck's cavity and tie the legs with string. Using a bamboo or metal skewer, poke holes in the skin, including the legs.

3 Place the duck, breast side down, on a rack over a roasting pan and cook it in the oven for 45 minutes, basting from time to time with the juices that have dripped into the pan. After 45 minutes, turn the duck over so that it is breast side up. Baste it generously and return it to the oven for a further 45 minutes, basting it every 15 minutes. The duck is ready once the juices run clear when the bird is pierced with a skewer.

4 Serve immediately, pulling at the skin and meat with your fingers, rather than neatly carving it. Serve with the plum sauce, pickled vegetables and salad leaves if using.

COOK'S TIP
Leaving the duck uncovered in the refrigerator for 24 hours will allow the skin to dry out thoroughly, ensuring that it becomes succulent and crispy when cooked.

SERVES SIX

INGREDIENTS
  1 duck, about 2.25kg/5lb
  90g/3½oz fresh root ginger, peeled, roughly chopped and lightly crushed
  4 garlic cloves, peeled and crushed
  1 lemon grass stalk, halved and bruised
  4 spring onions (scallions), halved and crushed
  plum dipping sauce, pickled vegetables and salad leaves, to serve (optional)
For the marinade
  80ml/3fl oz fish sauce
  30ml/2 tbsp soy sauce
  30ml/2 tbsp honey
  15ml/1 tbsp five-spice powder
  5ml/1 tsp ground ginger

1 In a bowl, beat the ingredients for the marinade together until well blended. Rub the skin of the duck lightly to loosen it, until you can get your fingers between the skin and the meat. Rub the marinade all over the duck, inside its skin and out, then place the duck on a rack over a tray and put it in the refrigerator for 24 hours.

Energy 210kcal/883kJ; Protein 27.4g; Carbohydrate 5.8g, of which sugars 4.5g; Fat 8.8g, of which saturates 2.7g, of which polyunsaturates 1.4g; Cholesterol 147mg; Calcium 35mg; Fibre 0.8g; Sodium 506mg.

DUCK WITH PINEAPPLE AND GINGER ★★

DUCK IS OFTEN THOUGHT OF AS A MEAT THAT IS HIGH IN FAT, BUT IN THIS RECIPE BONELESS DUCK BREAST FILLETS ARE SKINNED FOR A DISH THAT IS BURSTING WITH FLAVOUR AND LOW IN FAT.

SERVES THREE

INGREDIENTS
2 duck breast fillets
4 spring onions (scallions), chopped
15ml/1 tbsp light soy sauce
225g/8oz can pineapple rings
75ml/5 tbsp water
4 pieces drained stem ginger in
   syrup, plus 45ml/3 tbsp syrup
   from the jar
30ml/2 tbsp cornflour (cornstarch)
   mixed to a paste with a little water
1/4 each red and green (bell) pepper,
   seeded and cut into thin strips
salt and ground black pepper
cooked thin egg noodles, baby
   spinach and green beans, blanched,
   to serve

1 Strip the skin from the duck. Select a shallow bowl that will fit into your steamer and that will accommodate the duck fillets side by side. Spread out the chopped spring onions in the bowl, arrange the duck on top and cover with baking parchment. Set the steamer over boiling water and cook the duck for about 1 hour or until tender. Remove the duck from the steamer and leave to cool slightly.

2 Cut the duck fillets into thin slices. Place on a plate and moisten them with a little of the cooking juices from the steaming bowl. Strain the remaining juices into a small pan and set aside. Cover the duck slices with the baking parchment or foil and keep warm.

3 Drain the canned pineapple rings, reserving 75ml/5 tbsp of the juice. Add this to the reserved cooking juices in the pan, together with the measured water. Stir in the ginger syrup, then stir in the cornflour paste and cook, stirring until thickened. Season to taste.

4 Cut the pineapple and ginger into attractive shapes. Put the cooked noodles, baby spinach and green beans on a plate, add slices of duck and top with the pineapple, ginger and pepper strips. Pour over the sauce and serve.

Energy 253kcal/1071kJ; Protein 20.8g; Carbohydrate 33.1g, of which sugars 23.8g; Fat 6.8g, of which saturates 1.4g, of which polyunsaturates 0.7g; Cholesterol 110mg; Calcium 31mg; Fibre 1.1g; Sodium 515mg.

DRY-COOKED PORK STRIPS ★★

THIS TASTY DISH IS QUICK AND LIGHT ON A HOT DAY. PORK, CHICKEN, PRAWNS AND SQUID CAN ALL BE COOKED THIS WAY. WITH THE LETTUCE AND HERBS, IT'S A VERY FLAVOURSOME MEAL, BUT YOU CAN SERVE IT WITH JASMINE RICE AND A DIPPING SAUCE, IF YOU LIKE.

SERVES TWO

INGREDIENTS
15ml/1 tbsp sunflower oil
30ml/2 tbsp fish sauce
30ml/2 tbsp soy sauce
5ml/1 tsp sugar
225g/8oz lean pork fillet, cut into thin, bitesize strips
8 lettuce leaves
chilli sauce, for drizzling
fresh coriander (cilantro) leaves
a handful of fresh mint leaves

VARIATION
Try basil, flat leaf parsley, spring onions or sliced red onion in these parcels.

1 In a wok or heavy pan, heat the oil, fish sauce and soy sauce with the sugar. Add the pork and stir-fry over a medium heat, until all the liquid has evaporated. Cook the pork until it turns brown, almost caramelized, but not burnt.

2 Use a slotted spoon to lift the pork strips out of the wok. Drop spoonfuls of the cooked pork into lettuce leaves, drizzle a little chilli sauce over the top, add a few coriander and mint leaves, wrap them up and serve immediately.

Energy 104kcal/435kJ; Protein 12.5g; Carbohydrate 2.1g, of which sugars 2g; Fat 5.1g, of which saturates 1.2g, of which polyunsaturates 2.2g; Cholesterol 35mg; Calcium 13mg; Fibre 0.2g; Sodium 574mg.

CHA SHAO ★★

THIS DISH IS OFTEN KNOWN AS BARBECUE PORK AND IS VERY POPULAR THROUGHOUT SOUTH-EAST ASIA. THE NAME OF THIS DISH COMES FROM THE WAY IN WHICH IT WAS ORIGINALLY COOKED, CHA — BIG FORK, AND SHAO — TO COOK BY OPEN FIRE. SERVE IT WITH STEAMED RICE FOR A LOW-FAT MEAL.

SERVES SIX

INGREDIENTS
  900g/2lb lean pork fillet (tenderloin)
  15ml/1 tbsp clear honey
  45ml/3 tbsp rice wine or
    medium-dry sherry
  spring onion (scallion) curls,
    to garnish
For the marinade
  150ml/¼ pint/⅔ cup dark
    soy sauce
  90ml/6 tbsp rice wine or
    medium-dry sherry
  150ml/¼ pint/⅔ cup well-flavoured
    chicken stock
  15ml/1 tbsp soft brown sugar
  1cm/½in piece fresh root ginger,
    peeled and finely sliced
  40ml/2½ tbsp chopped onion

1 Mix all the marinade ingredients in a pan and stir over a medium heat until the mixture boils. Lower the heat and simmer gently for 15 minutes, stirring from time to time. Leave to cool.

2 Put the pork fillets in a shallow dish that is large enough to hold them side by side. Pour over 250ml/8fl oz/1 cup of the marinade, cover and chill for at least 8 hours, turning the meat over several times.

COOK'S TIP
You will have extra marinade when making this dish. Chill or freeze this and use to baste other grilled (broiled) dishes or meats, such as spare ribs.

3 Preheat the oven to 200°C/400°F/ Gas 6. Drain the pork fillets, reserving the marinade in the dish. Place the meat on a rack over a roasting pan and pour water into the pan to a depth of 1cm/½in. Place the pan in the oven and roast for 20 minutes.

4 Stir the honey and rice wine or sherry into the marinade. Remove the meat from the oven and place in the marinade, turning to coat. Put back on the rack and roast for 20–30 minutes or until cooked. Serve hot or cold, in slices, garnished with spring onion curls.

Energy 211kcal/886kJ; Protein 32.5g; Carbohydrate 4.8g, of which sugars 4.7g; Fat 6g, of which saturates 2.1g, of which polyunsaturates 1.1g; Cholesterol 95mg; Calcium 14mg; Fibre 0g; Sodium 996mg.

RICE ROLLS STUFFED WITH PORK ★

*IN THIS CLASSIC SOUTH-EAST ASIAN DISH, STEAMED RICE SHEETS ARE FILLED WITH MINCED PORK,
ROLLED UP AND THEN DIPPED IN A CHILLI SAUCE. SERVE WITH ANY OF THE VEGETARIAN SALADS IN
THE CHAPTER ON VEGETARIAN, SIDE DISHES AND SALADS FOR A HEALTHY LOW-FAT MEAL.*

SERVES SIX

INGREDIENTS
  25g/1oz dried cloud ear (wood ear)
    mushrooms, soaked in warm water
    for 30 minutes
  350g/12oz minced (ground) lean pork
  30nl/2 tbsp fish sauce
  10ml/2 tsp sugar
  15ml/1 tbsp sunflower oil
  2 garlic cloves, finely chopped
  2 shallots, finely chopped
  2 spring onions (scallions), trimmed
    and finely chopped
  24 fresh rice sheets, 7.5cm/3in square
  ground black pepper
  chilli sauce, or any other sauce
    for dipping

COOK'S TIP
To make life easy, prepared, fresh rice
sheets are available in Asian markets.

1 Drain the mushrooms and squeeze
out any excess water. Cut off and
discard the hard stems. Finely chop the
rest of the mushrooms and put them in
a bowl. Add the minced pork, fish
sauce, and sugar and mix well.

2 Heat the oil in a wok or heavy pan.
Add the garlic, shallots and onions. Stir-
fry until golden. Add the pork mixture
and stir-fry for 5–6 minutes, until the
pork is cooked. Season with pepper.

3 Place the fresh rice sheets on a flat
surface. Spoon a tablespoon of the
pork mixture on to the middle of each
sheet. Fold one side over the filling,
tuck in the sides, and roll up to
enclose the filling, so that it resembles
a short spring roll.

4 Place the filled rice rolls on a serving
plate and serve with any chilli or tangy
sauce of your choice, for dipping.

Energy 160kcal/670kJ; Protein 13.8g; Carbohydrate 16g, of which sugars 2.4g; Fat 4.4g, of which saturates 1.1g, of which polyunsaturates 1.6g; Cholesterol 37mg; Calcium 13mg; Fibre 0.6g; Sodium 43mg.

LEMON GRASS PORK ★★

CHILLIES AND LEMON GRASS FLAVOUR THIS SIMPLE STIR-FRY, WHILE PEANUTS ADD AN INTERESTING CONTRAST IN TEXTURE. LOOK FOR JARS OF CHOPPED LEMON GRASS, WHICH ARE HANDY WHEN THE FRESH VEGETABLE ISN'T AVAILABLE. THE PEANUTS ENRICH THE FLAVOUR WITHOUT SIGNIFICANTLY ADDING FAT.

SERVES FOUR

INGREDIENTS

  500g/1¼lb boneless pork loin
  2 lemon grass stalks,
    finely chopped
  4 spring onions (scallions),
    thinly sliced
  5ml/1 tsp salt
  12 black peppercorns,
    coarsely crushed
  15ml/1 tbsp sunflower oil
  2 garlic cloves, chopped
  2 fresh red chillies, seeded
    and chopped
  5ml/1 tsp soft light brown sugar
  30ml/2 tbsp Thai fish sauce
  30ml/2 tbsp roasted unsalted
    peanuts, chopped
  ground black pepper
  cooked rice noodles, to serve
  coarsely torn coriander (cilantro)
    leaves, to garnish

3 Add the garlic and red chillies and stir-fry for a further 5–8 minutes over a medium heat, until the pork is cooked through and tender.

4 Add the sugar, fish sauce and chopped peanuts and toss to mix, then season to taste with black pepper. Serve immediately on a bed of rice noodles, garnished with the coarsely torn coriander leaves.

COOK'S TIP
The heat in chillies is not in the seeds, but in the membranes surrounding them, which are removed along with the seeds.

1 Trim any excess fat from the pork. Cut the meat across into 5mm/¼in thick slices, then cut each slice into 5mm/¼in strips. Put the pork into a bowl with the finely chopped lemon grass, thinly sliced spring onions, salt and crushed peppercorns; mix well. Cover the bowl with clear film (plastic wrap) and leave to marinate in a cool place or the refrigerator for 30 minutes.

2 Preheat a wok, add the oil and swirl it around. Add the pork mixture and stir-fry over a medium heat for about 3 minutes, until browned all over.

Energy 205kcal/856kJ; Protein 27.9g; Carbohydrate 1.8g, of which sugars 1.6g; Fat 9.5g, of which saturates 2.4g, of which polyunsaturates 3.1g; Cholesterol 79mg; Calcium 16mg; Fibre 0.4g; Sodium 88mg.

CURRIED PORK WITH PICKLED GARLIC ★★

THIS VERY RICH CURRY IS BEST ACCOMPANIED BY LOTS OF PLAIN RICE AND PERHAPS A LIGHT VEGETABLE DISH. IT COULD SERVE FOUR IF SERVED WITH A VEGETABLE CURRY. IT IS WELL WORTH INVESTING IN A JAR OF PICKLED GARLIC FROM ASIAN STORES, AS THE TASTE IS SWEET AND DELICIOUS.

SERVES TWO

INGREDIENTS

130g/4½oz lean pork steaks
15ml/1 tbsp sunflower oil
1 garlic clove, crushed
15ml/1 tbsp Thai red curry paste
130ml/4½fl oz/generous ½ cup
  reduced-fat coconut milk
2.5cm/1in piece fresh root ginger,
  finely chopped
30ml/2 tbsp vegetable or
  chicken stock
30ml/2 tbsp fish sauce
5ml/1 tsp granulated sugar
2.5ml/½ tsp ground turmeric
10ml/2 tsp lemon juice
4 pickled garlic cloves,
  finely chopped
strips of lemon and lime rind,
  to garnish

1 Place the pork steaks in the freezer for 30–40 minutes, until firm, then, using a sharp knife, cut the meat into fine slivers, trimming off any excess fat.

2 Heat the oil in a wok or large, heavy frying pan and cook the garlic over a low to medium heat until golden brown. Do not let it burn. Add the curry paste and stir it in well.

3 Add the coconut milk and stir until the liquid begins to reduce and thicken. Stir in the pork. Cook for 2 minutes more, until the pork is cooked through.

4 Add the ginger, stock, fish sauce, sugar and turmeric, stirring constantly, then add the lemon juice and pickled garlic. Spoon into bowls, garnish with strips of rind, and serve.

Energy 160kcal/667kJ; Protein 14.9g; Carbohydrate 6g, of which sugars 5.9g; Fat 8.6g, of which saturates 1.7g, of which polyunsaturates 4g; Cholesterol 41mg; Calcium 75mg; Fibre 1.3g; Sodium 126mg.

SWEET AND SOUR PORK, THAI-STYLE ★

IT WAS THE CHINESE WHO ORIGINALLY CREATED SWEET AND SOUR COOKING, BUT THE THAIS ALSO DO IT VERY WELL. THIS VERSION HAS A FRESHER AND CLEANER FLAVOUR THAN THE ORIGINAL. IT MAKES A GOOD ONE-DISH MEAL WHEN SERVED OVER RICE.

SERVES FOUR

INGREDIENTS

350g/12oz lean pork
15ml/1 tbsp sunflower oil
4 garlic cloves, thinly sliced
1 small red onion, sliced
30ml/2 tbsp Thai fish sauce
15ml/1 tbsp granulated sugar
1 red (bell) pepper, seeded and diced
½ cucumber, seeded and sliced
2 plum tomatoes, cut into wedges
115g/4oz piece of fresh pineapple,
  cut into small chunks
2 spring onions (scallions), cut into
  short lengths
ground black pepper

To garnish
  coriander (cilantro) leaves
  spring onions (scallions), shredded

1 Place the pork in the freezer for 30–40 minutes, until firm. Using a sharp knife, cut it into thin strips.

2 Heat the oil in a wok or large frying pan. Add the garlic. Cook over a medium heat until golden, then add the pork and stir-fry for 4–5 minutes. Add the onion slices and toss to mix.

3 Add the fish sauce, sugar and ground black pepper to taste. Toss the mixture over the heat for 3–4 minutes more.

4 Stir in the red pepper, cucumber, tomatoes, pineapple and spring onions. Stir-fry for 3–4 minutes more, then spoon into a bowl. Garnish with the coriander and spring onions and serve.

Energy 168kcal/708kJ; Protein 20.3g; Carbohydrate 13.5g, of which sugars 12.9g; Fat 4g, of which saturates 1.3g, of which polyunsaturates 0.9g; Cholesterol 55mg; Calcium 32mg; Fibre 2g; Sodium 604mg.

BRAISED BLACK PEPPER PORK ★

THIS DISH IS QUICK, TASTY AND BEAUTIFULLY WARMING THANKS TO THE COMBINATION OF GINGER AND BLACK PEPPER. IT IS SURE TO BE A POPULAR CHOICE FOR A FAMILY MEAL.

SERVES SIX

INGREDIENTS
   1 litre/1¾ pints/4 cups water
   45ml/3 tbsp fish sauce
   30ml/2 tbsp soy sauce
   15ml/1 tbsp sugar
   4 garlic cloves, crushed
   40g/1½oz fresh root ginger, peeled
     and finely shredded
   15ml/1 tbsp freshly ground
     black pepper
   675g/1½lb lean pork shoulder or
     rump, cut into bitesize cubes
   steamed jasmine rice, crunchy salad
     and pickles or stir-fried greens,
     such as water spinach or long
     beans, to serve

1 In a large heavy pan, bring the water, fish sauce and soy sauce to the boil. Reduce the heat and stir in the sugar, garlic, ginger, black pepper and pork. Cover the pan and simmer for about 1½ hours, until the pork is very tender and the liquid has reduced.

2 Serve the pork in individual bowls with steamed jasmine rice. Drizzle the braised juices over it, and accompany it with a fresh crunchy salad, pickles or stir-fried greens, such as delicious stir-fried water spinach, or long beans.

Energy 154kcal/647kJ; Protein 24.4g; Carbohydrate 4g, of which sugars 3.7g; Fat 4.5g, of which saturates 1.6g, of which polyunsaturates 0.8g; Cholesterol 71mg; Calcium 13mg; Fibre 0.1g; Sodium 613mg.

GREEN BEEF CURRY WITH THAI AUBERGINES ★★

THIS IS A VERY QUICK CURRY SO BE SURE TO USE GOOD QUALITY MEAT. SIRLOIN STEAK IS RECOMMENDED, BUT TENDER RUMP STEAK COULD BE USED INSTEAD.

SERVES SIX

INGREDIENTS
    450g/1lb lean beef sirloin
    15ml/1 tbsp sunflower oil
    45ml/3 tbsp Thai green curry paste
    600ml/1 pint/2½ cups reduced-fat
        coconut milk
    4 kaffir lime leaves, torn
    15–30ml/1–2 tbsp fish sauce
    5ml/1 tsp palm sugar
    150g/5oz small Thai aubergines
        (eggplants), halved
    a small handful of fresh Thai basil
    2 fresh green chillies, to garnish

1 Trim off any excess fat from the beef. Using a sharp knife, cut it into long, thin strips. This is easiest to do if it is well chilled. Set it aside.

2 Heat the oil in a large, heavy pan or wok. Add the curry paste and cook for 1–2 minutes, until it is fragrant.

3 Stir in half the coconut milk, a little at a time. Cook, stirring frequently, for about 5–6 minutes, until an oily sheen appears on the surface of the liquid.

4 Add the beef to the pan with the kaffir lime leaves, Thai fish sauce, sugar and aubergine halves. Cook for 2–3 minutes, then stir in the remaining coconut milk.

5 Bring back to a simmer and cook until the meat and aubergines are tender. Stir in the Thai basil just before serving. Finely shred the green chillies and use to garnish the curry.

COOK'S TIP
To make the green curry paste, put 15 fresh green chillies, 2 chopped lemon grass stalks, 3 sliced shallots, 2 garlic cloves, 15ml/1 tbsp chopped galangal, 4 chopped kaffir lime leaves, 2.5ml/ ½ tsp grated kaffir lime rind, 5ml/1 tsp chopped coriander root, 6 black peppercorns, 5ml/1 tsp each roasted coriander and cumin seeds, 15ml/1 tbsp granulated sugar, 5ml/1 tsp salt and 5ml/1 tsp shrimp paste into a food processor and process until smooth. Gradually add 30ml/2 tbsp vegetable oil, processing after each addition.

Energy 174kcal/726kJ; Protein 17.6g; Carbohydrate 5.5g, of which sugars 5.4g; Fat 9.2g, of which saturates 3.3g, of which polyunsaturates 1.5g; Cholesterol 44mg; Calcium 35mg; Fibre 0.5g; Sodium 159mg.

LARP OF CHIANG MAI ★

CHIANG MAI IS A CITY IN THE NORTH-EAST OF THAILAND. THE CITY IS CULTURALLY VERY CLOSE TO LAOS AND FAMOUS FOR ITS CHICKEN SALAD, WHICH WAS ORIGINALLY CALLED "LAAP" OR "LARP". DUCK, BEEF OR PORK CAN BE USED INSTEAD OF CHICKEN.

SERVES FOUR

INGREDIENTS

450g/1lb minced (ground) chicken
    or pork
1 lemon grass stalk, root trimmed
3 kaffir lime leaves, finely chopped
4 fresh red chillies, seeded
    and chopped
60ml/4 tbsp lime juice
30ml/2 tbsp fish sauce
15ml/1 tbsp roasted ground rice (see
    Cook's Tip)
2 spring onions (scallions), chopped
30ml/2 tbsp fresh coriander
    (cilantro) leaves
thinly sliced kaffir lime leaves, mixed
    salad leaves and fresh mint sprigs,
    to garnish

1 Heat a large non-stick frying pan. Add the minced chicken or pork and moisten with a little water. Stir constantly over a medium heat for 7–10 minutes until it is cooked. Meanwhile, cut off the lower 5cm/2in of the lemon grass stalk and chop finely.

2 Transfer the cooked chicken to a bowl and add the chopped lemon grass, lime leaves, chillies, lime juice, fish sauce, ground rice, spring onions and coriander. Mix thoroughly.

3 Spoon the chicken mixture into a salad bowl. Sprinkle sliced kaffir lime leaves over the top and garnish with salad leaves and sprigs of mint.

COOK'S TIP
Use glutinous rice for the roasted ground rice. Put the rice in a frying pan and dry-fry it until golden brown. Remove and grind to a powder, using a pestle and mortar or a food processor. When the rice is cold, store it in a glass jar in a cool and dry place.

THAI BEEF SALAD ★★

A HEARTY AND HEALTHY MAIN MEAL SALAD, PACKED WITH GREEN VEGETABLES, THIS COMBINES TENDER STRIPS OF STEAK WITH A WONDERFUL CHILLI AND LIME DRESSING.

SERVES FOUR

INGREDIENTS

2 sirloin steaks, each
    about 400g/14oz
1 lemon grass stalk, root trimmed
1 red onion or 4 Thai shallots,
    thinly sliced
1/2 cucumber, cut into strips
30ml/2 tbsp chopped spring
    onion (scallion)
juice of 2 limes
15–30ml/1–2 tbsp fish sauce
Chinese mustard cress, salad
    cress, or fresh coriander (cilantro)
    to garnish

COOK'S TIP
Look out for gui chai leaves in Thai and Asian groceries. These look like very thin spring onions (scallions) and are often used as a substitute for the more familiar vegetable.

1 Pan-fry or grill (broil) the steaks in a large, heavy frying pan over a medium heat, for 6–8 minutes for medium-rare and about 10 minutes for well done. Remove from the pan and allow to rest for 10–15 minutes. Meanwhile, cut off the lower 5cm/2in from the lemon grass stalk and chop it finely.

2 When the meat is cool, slice it thinly and put the slices in a large bowl.

3 Add the sliced onion or shallots, cucumber, lemon grass and chopped spring onion to the meat slices.

4 Toss the salad and season with the lime juice and fish sauce to taste. Transfer the salad to a serving bowl or plate and serve at room temperature or chilled, garnished with the Chinese mustard cress, salad cress or coriander leaves.

Top: Energy 163kcal/682kJ; Protein 25.3g; Carbohydrate 4.4g, of which sugars 1.2g; Fat 4.8g, of which saturates 1.6g, of which polyunsaturates 0.8g; Cholesterol 71mg; Calcium 53mg; Fibre 1.1g; Sodium 620mg.
Bottom: Energy 186kcal/774kJ; Protein 23.3g; Carbohydrate 2g, of which sugars 1.6g; Fat 9.4g, of which saturates 3.8g, of which polyunsaturates 0.4g; Cholesterol 58mg; Calcium 16mg; Fibre 0.4g; Sodium 333mg.

BEEF STEW <u>WITH</u> STAR ANISE ★★★

NOT A WESTERN IDEA OF A STEW, BUT MORE OF A FRAGRANT SOUP WITH TENDER MORSELS OF BEEF. THE BEANSPROUTS, SPRING ONION AND CORIANDER ARE ADDED AT THE END OF COOKING FOR A DELIGHTFUL AND HEALTHY CONTRAST IN TASTE AND TEXTURE.

SERVES FOUR

INGREDIENTS
1 litre/1¾ pints/4 cups vegetable or
  chicken stock
450g/1lb beef steak, cut into slivers
3 garlic cloves, finely chopped
3 coriander (cilantro) roots,
  finely chopped
2 cinnamon sticks
4 star anise
30ml/2 tbsp light soy sauce
30ml/2 tbsp fish sauce
5ml/1 tsp granulated sugar
115g/4oz/1⅓ cups beansprouts
1 spring onion (scallion),
  finely chopped
small bunch fresh coriander
  (cilantro), coarsely chopped

1 Pour the stock into a large, heavy pan. Add the beef, garlic, chopped coriander roots, cinnamon sticks, star anise, soy sauce, fish sauce and sugar. Bring to the boil, then reduce the heat to low and simmer for 30 minutes. Skim off any foam that rises to the surface of the liquid with a slotted spoon.

2 Meanwhile, divide the beansprouts among four individual serving bowls. Remove and discard the cinnamon sticks and star anise from the stew with a slotted spoon. Ladle the stew over the beansprouts, garnish with the chopped spring onion and chopped fresh coriander and serve immediately.

Energy 221kcal/923kJ; Protein 27.3g; Carbohydrate 4.1g, of which sugars 2.4g; Fat 10.7g, of which saturates 4.3g, of which polyunsaturates 0.5g; Cholesterol 65mg; Calcium 16mg; Fibre 0.8g; Sodium 608mg.

STIR-FRIED BEEF IN OYSTER SAUCE ★★

HERE IS ANOTHER SIMPLE BUT DELICIOUS CHINESE RECIPE. IN THAILAND THIS IS OFTEN MADE WITH JUST STRAW MUSHROOMS, WHICH ARE READILY AVAILABLE FRESH, BUT OYSTER MUSHROOMS MAKE A GOOD SUBSTITUTE AND USING A MIXTURE MAKES THE DISH EXTRA INTERESTING.

SERVES SIX

INGREDIENTS
- 450g/1lb rump (round) steak
- 30ml/2 tbsp soy sauce
- 15ml/1 tbsp cornflour (cornstarch)
- 15ml/1 tbsp sunflower oil
- 15ml/1 tbsp chopped garlic
- 15ml/1 tbsp chopped fresh root ginger
- 225g/8oz/3¼ cups mixed mushrooms such as shiitake, oyster and straw
- 30ml/2 tbsp oyster sauce
- 5ml/1 tsp granulated sugar
- 4 spring onions (scallions), cut into short lengths
- ground black pepper
- 2 fresh red chillies, seeded and cut into strips, to garnish

1 Place the steak in the freezer for 30–40 minutes, until firm, then, using a sharp knife, slice it on the diagonal into long thin strips.

2 Mix together the soy sauce and cornflour in a large bowl. Add the steak, turning to coat well, cover with clear film (plastic wrap) and leave to marinate at room temperature for 1–2 hours.

3 Heat half the oil in a wok or large, heavy frying pan. Add the garlic and ginger and cook for 1–2 minutes, until fragrant. Drain the steak, add it to the wok or pan and stir well to separate the strips. Cook, stirring frequently, for a further 1–2 minutes, until the steak is browned all over and tender. Remove from the wok or pan and set aside.

4 Heat the remaining oil in the wok or pan. Add the shiitake, oyster and straw mushrooms. Stir-fry over a medium heat until golden brown.

5 Return the steak to the wok and mix it with the mushrooms. Spoon in the oyster sauce and sugar, mix well, then add ground black pepper to taste. Toss over the heat until all the ingredients are thoroughly combined.

6 Stir in the spring onions. Tip the mixture on to a serving platter, garnish with the strips of red chilli and serve.

Energy 174kcal/725kJ; Protein 18.1g; Carbohydrate 5.2g, of which sugars 2.7g; Fat 9.1g, of which saturates 3.1g, of which polyunsaturates 1.6g; Cholesterol 44mg; Calcium 11mg; Fibre 0.6g; Sodium 489mg.

VEGETARIAN, SIDE DISHES AND SALADS

The wide range of different vegetables cooked together with the wonderful flavourings of exotic herbs, spices and sauces, makes Asian cooking a real pleasure for vegetarians. There are many exciting dishes to try, such as Green Papaya Salad, Stuffed Sweet Peppers, and Pineapple with Ginger and Chilli. An added attraction is that most of these dishes are very quick and easy to make.

STUFFED SWEET PEPPERS ★

THIS IS AN UNUSUAL RECIPE IN THAT THE STUFFED PEPPERS ARE STEAMED RATHER THAN BAKED. THE FILLING INCORPORATES TYPICAL THAI INGREDIENTS SUCH AS RED CURRY PASTE AND KAFFIR LIME LEAVES.

SERVES FOUR

INGREDIENTS
3 garlic cloves, finely chopped
2 coriander (cilantro) roots,
 finely chopped
400g/14oz/3 cups
 mushrooms, quartered
5ml/1 tsp Thai vegetarian red
 curry paste
1 egg, lightly beaten
15ml/1 tbsp light soy sauce
2.5ml/½ tsp granulated sugar
3 kaffir lime leaves, finely chopped
4 yellow (bell) peppers, halved
 lengthways and seeded

VARIATIONS
For extra colour use red or orange (bell) peppers if you prefer, or a combination of the two.

1 In a mortar or spice grinder pound or blend the garlic with the coriander roots. Scrape into a bowl.

2 Put the mushrooms in a food processor and pulse briefly until they are finely chopped. Add to the garlic and coriander mixture, then stir in the curry paste, egg, soy sauce, sugar and lime leaves.

3 Place the pepper halves in a single layer in two steamer baskets. Spoon the mushroom mixture loosely into the pepper halves. Do not pack the mixture down tightly or the filling will dry out too much. Bring the water in the steamer to the boil, then lower the heat to a simmer. Steam the peppers for 15 minutes, or until the flesh is tender. Serve hot.

Energy 95kcal/399kJ; Protein 5.6g; Carbohydrate 12.8g, of which sugars 12g; Fat 2.8g, of which saturates 0.7g, of which polyunsaturates 0.8g; Cholesterol 48mg; Calcium 53mg; Fibre 4.5g; Sodium 301mg.

GLAZED PUMPKIN <u>IN</u> COCONUT MILK ★

THROUGHOUT SOUTH-EAST ASIA, VARIATIONS OF THIS SWEET, MELLOW DISH ARE SERVED AS A MAIN COURSE. BUTTERNUT SQUASH AND WINTER MELONS CAN ALL BE COOKED IN THIS WAY.

SERVES FOUR

INGREDIENTS

200ml/7fl oz/scant 1 cup
  reduced-fat coconut milk
15ml/1 tbsp *kroeung*
30ml/2 tbsp palm sugar
15ml/1 tbsp sunflower oil
4 garlic cloves, finely chopped
25g/1oz fresh root ginger, peeled and
  finely shredded
675g/1½lb pumpkin flesh, cubed
ground black pepper
a handful of curry or basil leaves,
  to garnish
fried onion rings, to garnish
plain rice, to serve

1 In a bowl, beat the coconut milk and the *kroeung* with the sugar, until it has dissolved. Set aside.

2 Heat the oil in a wok or heavy pan and stir in the garlic and ginger.

3 Stir-fry the garlic and the ginger until they begin to colour, then stir in the pumpkin cubes, mixing well.

4 Pour in the reduced-fat coconut milk and mix well. Reduce the heat, cover and simmer for about 20 minutes, until the pumpkin is tender and the sauce has reduced. Season with ground black pepper and garnish with curry or basil leaves and fried onion rings. Serve hot with plain rice.

COOK'S TIP

Kroeung is a herb paste made from a blend of lemon grass, galangal, garlic and turmeric.

Energy 92kcal/386kJ; Protein 1.8g; Carbohydrate 14.4g, of which sugars 13.5g; Fat 3.4g, of which saturates 0.6g, of which polyunsaturates 1.8g; Cholesterol 0mg; Calcium 93mg; Fibre 2.3g; Sodium 60mg.

SWEET AND SOUR VEGETABLES WITH TOFU ★

BIG, BOLD AND BEAUTIFUL, THIS IS A HEARTY STIR-FRY THAT WILL SATISFY THE HUNGRIEST GUESTS. IT IS PACKED WITH COLOURFUL VEGETABLES INCLUDING CORN COBS, RED PEPPERS AND GREEN MANGETOUTS.

SERVES FOUR

INGREDIENTS

4 shallots
3 garlic cloves
15ml/1 tbsp sunflower oil
250g/9oz Chinese leaves (Chinese cabbage), shredded
8 baby corn cobs, sliced on the diagonal
2 red (bell) peppers, seeded and thinly sliced
200g/7oz/1¾ cups mangetouts (snow peas), trimmed and sliced
250g/9oz tofu, rinsed, drained and cut in 1cm/½in cubes
60ml/4 tbsp vegetable stock
30ml/2 tbsp light soy sauce
15ml/1 tbsp granulated sugar
30ml/2 tbsp rice vinegar
2.5ml/½ tsp dried chilli flakes
small bunch coriander (cilantro), chopped

1 Slice the shallots thinly using a sharp knife. Finely chop the garlic.

2 Heat the oil in a wok or large frying pan and cook the shallots and garlic for 2–3 minutes over a medium heat, until golden. Do not let the garlic burn or it will taste bitter.

3 Add the shredded cabbage, toss over the heat for 30 seconds, then add the corn cobs and repeat the process.

4 Add the red peppers, mangetouts and tofu in the same way, each time adding a single ingredient and tossing it over the heat for about 30 seconds before adding the next ingredient.

5 Pour in the stock and soy sauce. Mix together the sugar and vinegar in a small bowl, stirring until the sugar has dissolved, then add to the wok or pan. Sprinkle over the chilli flakes and coriander, toss to mix well and serve.

Energy 144kcal/604kJ; Protein 5.2g; Carbohydrate 23.7g, of which sugars 18.2g; Fat 3.7g, of which saturates 0.5g, of which polyunsaturates 2.2g; Cholesterol 0mg; Calcium 73mg; Fibre 4.7g; Sodium 611mg.

SPICY TOFU WITH BASIL AND PEANUTS ★★

AROMATIC PEPPER LEAVES ARE OFTEN USED AS THE HERB ELEMENT IN THAILAND BUT, BECAUSE THESE ARE QUITE DIFFICULT TO FIND OUTSIDE SOUTH-EAST ASIA, YOU CAN USE BASIL LEAVES INSTEAD.

SERVES FOUR

INGREDIENTS
    3 lemon grass stalks, finely chopped
    45ml/3 tbsp soy sauce
    2 red Serrano chillies, seeded and
      finely chopped
    2 garlic cloves, crushed
    5ml/1 tsp ground turmeric
    10ml/2 tsp sugar
    300g/11oz tofu, rinsed, drained,
      patted dry and cut into
      bitesize cubes
    15ml/1 tbsp sunflower oil
    15ml/1 tbsp roasted peanuts,
      chopped
    1 bunch fresh basil, stalks removed
    salt

1 In a bowl, mix together the lemon grass, soy sauce, chillies, garlic, turmeric and sugar until the sugar has dissolved. Add a little salt to taste and add the tofu, making sure it is well coated. Leave to marinate for 1 hour.

VARIATION
Replace the fresh basil with kaffir lime leaves, coriander (cilantro) leaves or curry leaves, all of which would work well in this simple stir-fry.

2 Heat a wok or heavy pan. Pour in the oil, add the marinated tofu, and cook, stirring frequently, until it is golden brown on all sides. Add the peanuts and most of the basil leaves.

3 Divide the marinated tofu and peanut mixture among individual serving dishes. Then sprinkle the remaining basil leaves over the top and serve hot or at room temperature.

Energy 115kcal/480kJ; Protein 7.4g; Carbohydrate 4.5g, of which sugars 3.9g; Fat 7.6g, of which saturates 1g, of which polyunsaturates 3.7g; Cholesterol 0mg; Calcium 388mg; Fibre 0.2g; Sodium 804mg.

TOFU AND GREEN BEAN RED CURRY ★

THIS IS ONE OF THOSE VERSATILE RECIPES THAT SHOULD BE IN EVERY COOK'S REPERTOIRE. THIS VERSION USES GREEN BEANS, BUT OTHER TYPES OF VEGETABLE WORK EQUALLY WELL. THE LOW-FAT TOFU TAKES ON THE FLAVOUR OF THE SPICE PASTE AND ALSO BOOSTS THE NUTRITIONAL VALUE.

SERVES FOUR

INGREDIENTS

200ml/7fl oz/scant 1 cup reduced-fat coconut milk
15ml/1 tbsp Thai vegetarian red curry paste
10ml/2 tsp palm sugar or light muscovado (brown) sugar
225g/8oz/3¼ cups button (white) mushrooms
400ml/14fl oz/1⅔ cups vegetable stock
115g/4oz/1 cup green beans, trimmed
175g/6oz firm tofu, rinsed, drained and cut in 2cm/¾ in cubes
4 kaffir lime leaves, torn
2 fresh red chillies, seeded and sliced
fresh coriander (cilantro) leaves, to garnish

1 Pour the reduced-fat coconut milk into a wok or pan. Cook until the coconut milk starts to separate and an oily sheen appears on the surface.

2 Add the red curry paste and sugar to the coconut milk. Mix thoroughly, then add the mushrooms. Stir and cook for 1 minute.

3 Stir in the stock. Bring back to the boil, then add the green beans and tofu cubes. Simmer gently for 4–5 minutes more.

4 Stir in the kaffir lime leaves and sliced red chillies. Spoon the curry into a serving dish, garnish with the coriander leaves and serve immediately.

Energy 67kcal/282kJ; Protein 5.3g; Carbohydrate 6.5g, of which sugars 6g; Fat 2.4g, of which saturates 0.4g, of which polyunsaturates 1.1g; Cholesterol 0mg; Calcium 253mg; Fibre 1.3g; Sodium 60mg.

SNAKE BEANS <u>WITH</u> TOFU ★★

ANOTHER NAME FOR SNAKE BEANS IS YARD-LONG BEANS. THIS IS SOMETHING OF AN EXAGGERATION BUT THEY DO GROW TO LENGTHS OF 40CM/16IN AND MORE. LOOK FOR THEM IN ASIAN STORES AND MARKETS, BUT IF YOU CAN'T FIND ANY, SUBSTITUTE OTHER GREEN BEANS.

SERVES FOUR

INGREDIENTS

500g/1¼lb long beans, thinly sliced
200g/7oz silken tofu, cut into cubes
2 shallots, thinly sliced
200ml/7fl oz/scant 1 cup reduced-fat
  coconut milk
25g/1oz roasted peanuts, chopped
juice of 1 lime
10ml/2 tsp palm sugar or light
  muscovado (brown) sugar
60ml/4 tbsp soy sauce
5ml/1 tsp dried chilli flakes

VARIATIONS

The sauce also works very well with mangetouts (snow peas). Alternatively, for a brightly coloured variation, stir in sliced yellow or red (bell) pepper.

1 Bring a pan of lightly salted water to the boil. Add the beans and blanch them for 30 seconds.

2 Drain the beans immediately, then refresh under cold water and drain again, shaking well to remove as much water as possible. Place in a serving bowl and set aside.

3 Put the tofu and shallots in a pan with the coconut milk. Heat gently, stirring, until the tofu begins to crumble.

4 Add the peanuts, lime juice, sugar, soy sauce and chilli flakes. Heat, stirring, until the sugar has dissolved. Pour the sauce over the beans, toss to combine and serve immediately.

Energy 167kcal/697kJ; Protein 9.9g; Carbohydrate 12.9g, of which sugars 9.3g; Fat 10g, of which saturates 1g, of which polyunsaturates 2.2g; Cholesterol 7mg; Calcium 327mg; Fibre 3.4g; Sodium 191mg.

PLAIN NOODLES <u>WITH</u> FOUR FLAVOURS ★

A WONDERFULLY SIMPLE WAY OF SERVING NOODLES, THIS DISH ALLOWS EACH INDIVIDUAL DINER TO SEASON THEIR OWN, SPRINKLING OVER THE FOUR FLAVOURS AS THEY LIKE. FLAVOURINGS ARE ALWAYS PUT OUT IN LITTLE BOWLS WHENEVER NOODLES ARE SERVED.

<u>SERVES FOUR</u>

INGREDIENTS
    4 small fresh red or green chillies
    60ml/4 tbsp fish sauce
    60ml/4 tbsp rice vinegar
    granulated sugar
    mild or hot chilli powder
    350g/12oz rice noodles

1 Prepare the four flavours. For the first, finely chop 2 small red or green chillies, discarding the seeds or leaving them in, depending on how hot you like your flavouring. Place them in a small bowl and add the fish sauce.

2 For the second flavour, chop the remaining chillies finely and mix them with the rice vinegar in a small bowl. Put the sugar and chilli powder in separate small bowls.

3 Cook the noodles until tender, following the instructions on the packet. Drain well, tip into a large bowl and serve immediately with the four flavours handed separately.

Energy 321kcal/1341kJ; Protein 4.5g; Carbohydrate 72.4g, of which sugars 1g; Fat 0.2g, of which saturates 0g, of which polyunsaturates 0g; Cholesterol 0mg; Calcium 12mg; Fibre 0.2g; Sodium 278mg.

THAI NOODLES <u>WITH</u> CHINESE CHIVES ★★

THIS RECIPE REQUIRES A LITTLE TIME FOR PREPARATION, BUT THE COOKING TIME IS VERY FAST.
EVERYTHING IS COOKED IN A HOT WOK AND SHOULD BE EATEN IMMEDIATELY. THIS IS A FILLING
AND TASTY VEGETARIAN DISH, IDEAL FOR A WEEKEND LUNCH.

SERVES FOUR

INGREDIENTS

   350g/12oz dried rice noodles
   1cm/½in piece fresh root ginger,
     peeled and grated
   30ml/2 tbsp light soy sauce
   225g/8oz Quorn (mycoprotein),
     cut into small cubes
   15ml/1 tbsp sunflower oil
   2 garlic cloves, crushed
   1 large onion, cut into
     thin wedges
   115g/4oz fried tofu, thinly sliced
   1 fresh green chilli, seeded and
     thinly sliced
   175g/6oz/2 cups beansprouts
   2 large bunches garlic chives, total
     weight about 115g/4oz, cut into
     5cm/2in lengths
   30ml/2 tbsp roasted peanuts, ground
   30ml/2 tbsp dark soy sauce
   30ml/2 tbsp chopped fresh coriander
     (cilantro), and 1 lemon, cut into
     wedges, to garnish

1 Place the noodles in a bowl, cover with warm water and leave to soak for 30 minutes. Drain and set aside.

2 Mix the ginger and light soy sauce in a bowl. Add the Quorn, then set aside for 10 minutes. Drain, reserving the marinade.

3 Heat half the oil in a frying pan and cook the garlic for a few seconds. Add the Quorn and stir-fry for 3–4 minutes. Using a slotted spoon, transfer to a plate and set aside.

4 Heat the remaining oil in the pan and stir-fry the onion for 3–4 minutes, until softened and tinged with brown. Add the tofu and chilli, stir-fry briefly and then add the noodles. Stir-fry over a medium heat for 4–5 minutes.

5 Stir in the beansprouts, garlic chives and most of the ground peanuts, reserving a little for the garnish. Stir well, then add the Quorn, the dark soy sauce and the reserved marinade.

6 When hot, spoon on to serving plates and garnish with the remaining ground peanuts, the coriander and lemon.

Energy 444kcal/1857kJ; Protein 16g; Carbohydrate 77.6g, of which sugars 4.3g; Fat 6.5g, of which saturates 0.9g, of which polyunsaturates 3.2g; Cholesterol 0mg; Calcium 230mg; Fibre 5g; Sodium 1227mg.

COCONUT RICE ★

THIS WAY OF COOKING RICE IS VERY POPULAR THROUGHOUT THE WHOLE OF SOUTH-EAST ASIA.
COCONUT RICE GOES PARTICULARLY WELL WITH FISH, CHICKEN AND PORK.

2 Lift the lid and check that all the liquid has been absorbed, then fork the rice through carefully, removing the cinnamon stick, lemon grass and bay leaf.

3 Cover the pan with a tight-fitting lid and continue to cook the rice over the lowest possible heat for 3–5 minutes more. Take care that the pan does not scorch.

4 Pile the rice on to a warm serving dish and serve garnished with the crisp fried onions.

SERVES SIX

INGREDIENTS
350g/12oz/1¾ cups Thai fragrant rice
400ml/14fl oz can reduced-fat
  coconut milk
300ml/½ pint/1¼ cups water
2.5ml/½ tsp ground coriander
5cm/2in cinnamon stick
1 lemon grass stalk, bruised
1 bay leaf
salt
crisp fried onions, to garnish

1 Put the rice in a strainer and rinse thoroughly under cold water. Drain well, then put in a pan. Pour in the coconut milk and water. Add the coriander, cinnamon stick, lemon grass and bay leaf. Season with salt. Bring to the boil, then lower the heat, cover and simmer for 8–10 minutes.

VARIATION
For a quick and easy healthy supper, stir in strips of freshly cooked skinless chicken breast and peas 5-6 minutes before serving and heat through.

Energy 226kcal/945kJ; Protein 4.6g; Carbohydrate 49.9g, of which sugars 3.4g; Fat 0.6g, of which saturates 0.1g, of which polyunsaturates 0g; Cholesterol 0mg; Calcium 39mg; Fibre 0.2g; Sodium 75mg.

BROWN RICE <u>WITH</u> LIME <u>AND</u> LEMON GRASS ★

IT IS UNUSUAL TO FIND BROWN RICE GIVEN THE THAI TREATMENT, BUT THE NUTTY FLAVOUR OF THE GRAINS IS ENHANCED BY THE FRAGRANCE OF LIMES AND LEMON GRASS IN THIS DELICIOUS DISH.

SERVES FOUR

INGREDIENTS
- 2 limes
- 1 lemon grass stalk
- 225g/8oz/generous 1 cup brown long grain rice
- 15ml/1 tbsp olive oil
- 1 onion, chopped
- 2.5cm/1in piece fresh root ginger, peeled and finely chopped
- 7.5ml/1½ tsp coriander seeds
- 7.5ml/1½ tsp cumin seeds
- 750ml/1¼ pints/3 cups vegetable stock
- 60ml/4 tbsp chopped fresh coriander (cilantro)
- spring onion (scallion) green and toasted coconut strips, to garnish
- lime wedges, to serve

1 Pare the limes, using a cannelle knife (zester) or fine grater, taking care to avoid cutting the bitter pith. Set the rind aside. Finely chop the lower portion of the lemon grass stalk and set it aside.

2 Rinse the rice in plenty of cold water until the water runs clear. Tip it into a sieve and drain thoroughly.

3 Heat the oil in a large pan. Add the onion, ginger, coriander and cumin seeds, lemon grass and lime rind and cook over a low heat for 2–3 minutes.

4 Add the rice to the pan and cook, stirring constantly, for 1 minute, then pour in the stock and bring to the boil. Reduce the heat to very low and cover the pan. Cook gently for 30 minutes, then check the rice. If it is still crunchy, cover the pan and cook for 3–5 minutes more. Remove from the heat.

5 Stir in the fresh coriander, fluff up the rice grains with a fork, cover the pan and leave to stand for 10 minutes. Transfer to a warmed dish, garnish with spring onion green and toasted coconut strips, and serve with lime wedges.

Energy 235kcal/996kJ; Protein 4.3g; Carbohydrate 47.3g, of which sugars 1.9g; Fat 4.5g, of which saturates 0.8g, of which polyunsaturates 0.8g; Cholesterol 0mg; Calcium 35mg; Fibre 1.9g; Sodium 6mg.

STIR-FRIED ASPARAGUS WITH CHILLI, GALANGAL AND LEMON GRASS ★

ONE OF THE CULINARY LEGACIES OF FRENCH COLONIZATION IN VIETNAM AND CAMBODIA IS ASPARAGUS. TODAY IT IS GROWN IN VIETNAM AND FINDS ITS WAY INTO STIR-FRIES IN COUNTRIES THROUGHOUT SOUTH-EAST ASIA. THIS IS A LOVELY WAY TO EAT ASPARAGUS.

SERVES FOUR

INGREDIENTS

15ml/1 tbsp sunfllower oil
2 garlic cloves, finely chopped
2 Thai chillies, seeded and finely
  chopped
25g/1oz galangal, finely shredded
1 lemon grass stalk, trimmed and
  finely sliced
350g/12oz fresh asparagus stalks,
  trimmed
30ml/2 tbsp fish sauce
30ml/2 tbsp soy sauce
5ml/1 tsp sugar
15ml/1 tbsp unsalted roasted
  peanuts, finely chopped
1 small bunch fresh coriander
  (cilantro), finely chopped

1 Heat a large wok and add the oil. Stir in the garlic, chillies, galangal and lemon grass and stir-fry until they become fragrant and begin to turn golden.

2 Add the asparagus and stir-fry for a further 1–2 minutes, until it is just tender but not too soft.

3 Stir in the fish sauce, soy sauce and sugar. Stir in the peanuts and coriander and serve immediately.

VARIATION
This recipe also works well with broccoli, green beans and courgettes (zucchini), cut into strips.

Energy 79kcal/327kJ; Protein 4g; Carbohydrate 4.9g, of which sugars 4.5g; Fat 4.9g, of which saturates 0.7g, of which polyunsaturates 2.3g; Cholesterol 0mg; Calcium 53mg; Fibre 2.5g; Sodium 540mg.

STEAMED VEGETABLES WITH CHIANG MAI SPICY DIP ★

IN THAILAND, STEAMED VEGETABLES ARE OFTEN PARTNERED WITH RAW ONES TO CREATE THE CONTRASTING TEXTURES THAT ARE SUCH A FEATURE OF THE NATIONAL CUISINE. BY HAPPY COINCIDENCE, IT IS AN EXTREMELY HEALTHY WAY TO SERVE THEM.

SERVES FOUR

INGREDIENTS
 1 head broccoli, divided
   into florets
 130g/4½oz 1 cup green
   beans, trimmed
 130g/4½oz asparagus, trimmed
 ½ head cauliflower, divided
   into florets
 8 baby corn cobs
 130g/4½oz mangetouts (snow peas)
   or sugar snap peas
 salt
For the dip
 1 fresh green chilli, seeded
 4 garlic cloves, peeled
 4 shallots, peeled
 2 tomatoes, halved
 5 pea aubergines (eggplants)
 30ml/2 tbsp lemon juice
 30ml/2 tbsp soy sauce
 2.5ml/½ tsp salt
 5ml/1 tsp granulated sugar

COOK'S TIP
Cauliflower varieties with pale green florets have a more delicate flavour than those with white florets.

1 Place the broccoli, green beans, asparagus and cauliflower in a steamer and steam over boiling water for about 4 minutes, until just tender but still with a "bite". Transfer them to a bowl and add the corn cobs and mangetouts or sugar snap peas. Season to taste with a little salt. Toss to mix, then set aside.

2 Make the dip. Preheat the grill (broiler). Wrap the chilli, garlic cloves, shallots, tomatoes and aubergines in a foil package. Grill (broil) for 10 minutes, until the vegetables have softened, turning the package over once or twice.

3 Unwrap the foil and tip its contents into a mortar or food processor. Add the lemon juice, soy sauce, salt and sugar. Pound with a pestle or process to a fairly liquid paste.

4 Scrape the dip into a serving bowl or four individual bowls. Serve, surrounded by the steamed and raw vegetables.

VARIATIONS
You can use a combination of other vegetables if you like. Use pak choi (bok choy) instead of the cauliflower or substitute raw baby carrots for the corn cobs and mushrooms in place of the mangetouts (snow peas).

Energy 101kcal/422kJ; Protein 9.5g; Carbohydrate 11.9g, of which sugars 10.2g; Fat 2g, of which saturates 0.4g, of which polyunsaturates 1g; Cholesterol 0mg; Calcium 98mg; Fibre 6.7g; Sodium 1082mg.

MORNING GLORY WITH GARLIC AND SHALLOTS ★

WATER MORNING GLORY GOES BY VARIOUS NAMES, INCLUDING WATER SPINACH, WATER CONVOLVULUS AND SWAMP CABBAGE. IT IS A GREEN LEAFY VEGETABLE WITH LONG JOINTED STEMS AND ARROW-SHAPED LEAVES. THE STEMS REMAIN CRUNCHY WHILE THE LEAVES WILT LIKE SPINACH WHEN COOKED.

SERVES FOUR

INGREDIENTS

2 bunches water morning glory, total
   weight about 250g/9oz, trimmed
   and coarsely chopped into 2.5cm/
   1in lengths
15ml/1 tbsp sunflower oil
4 shallots, thinly sliced
6 large garlic cloves, thinly sliced
sea salt
1.5ml/¼ tsp dried chilli flakes

VARIATIONS
Use spinach instead of morning glory, or
substitute young spring greens (collards),
sprouting broccoli or Swiss chard.

1 Place the water morning glory in a
steamer and steam over a pan of boiling
water for 30 seconds, until just wilted. If
necessary, cook it in batches. Place the
leaves in a bowl or spread them out on
a large serving plate.

2 Heat the oil in a wok and stir-fry the
shallots and garlic over a medium to
high heat until golden. Spoon the
mixture over the morning glory, sprinkle
with a little sea salt and the chilli flakes
and serve immediately.

Energy 58kcal/240kJ; Protein 2.9g; Carbohydrate 4.2g, of which sugars 2g; Fat 3.4g, of which saturates 0.4g, of which polyunsaturates 2.1g; Cholesterol 0mg; Calcium 113mg; Fibre 2g; Sodium 89mg.

STIR-FRIED PINEAPPLE WITH GINGER ★

THIS DISH MAKES AN INTERESTING ACCOMPANIMENT TO GRILLED MEAT OR STRONGLY FLAVOURED FISH SUCH AS TUNA OR SWORDFISH. IF THE IDEA SEEMS STRANGE, THINK OF IT AS RESEMBLING A FRESH MANGO CHUTNEY, BUT WITH PINEAPPLE AS THE PRINCIPAL INGREDIENT.

SERVES FOUR

INGREDIENTS
1 pineapple
15ml/1 tbsp sunflower oil
2 garlic cloves, finely chopped
2 shallots, finely chopped
5cm/2in piece fresh root ginger, peeled and finely shredded
30ml/2 tbsp light soy sauce
juice of ½ lime
1 large fresh red chilli, seeded and finely shredded

VARIATION
This also tastes excellent if peaches or nectarines are substituted for the diced pineapple. Use three or four, depending on their size.

1 Trim and peel the pineapple. Cut out the core and dice the flesh.

2 Heat the oil in a wok or frying pan. Stir-fry the garlic and shallots over a medium heat for 2–3 minutes, until golden. Do not let the garlic burn or the dish will taste bitter.

3 Add the pineapple. Stir-fry for about 2 minutes, or until the pineapple cubes start to turn golden on the edges.

4 Add the ginger, soy sauce, lime juice and chopped chilli. Toss together until well mixed. Cook over a low heat for a further 2 minutes, then serve.

Energy 119kcal/507kJ; Protein 1.3g; Carbohydrate 22.8g, of which sugars 22.4g; Fat 3.2g, of which saturates 0.4g, of which polyunsaturates 2g; Cholesterol 0mg; Calcium 42mg; Fibre 2.8g; Sodium 539mg.

FRIED VEGETABLES ★★

NAM PRIK IS THE UNIVERSAL THAI FISH SAUCE. IT CAN BE SERVED AS A CONDIMENT, BUT IT IS
MORE OFTEN USED AS A DIP FOR FRESH OR COOKED VEGETABLES.

SERVES SIX

INGREDIENTS

3 large (US extra large) eggs
1 aubergine (eggplant), halved
  lengthways and cut into long,
  thin slices
½ small butternut squash,
  peeled, seeded and cut into
  long, thin slices
2 courgettes (zucchini),
  trimmed and cut into long,
  thin slices
75ml/5 tbsp sunflower oil
salt and ground black pepper
nam prik or sweet chilli
  sauce, to serve (see
  Cook's Tip)

1 Beat the eggs in a large bowl. Add the aubergine, butternut squash and courgette slices. Toss the vegetables until coated all over in the egg, then season with salt and pepper.

2 Heat the oil in a wok. When it is hot, add the vegetables, one strip at a time, making sure that each strip has plenty of egg clinging to it. Do not cook more than eight strips at a time or the oil will cool down too much.

COOK'S TIP
Nam prik is quite a complex sauce, numbering dried shrimp, tiny aubergines (eggplant), shrimp paste and lime or lemon juice among its ingredients.

3 As each strip turns golden and is cooked, lift it out, using a wire basket or slotted spoon, and drain on kitchen paper. Keep hot while cooking the remaining vegetables. Transfer to a warmed dish and serve with the *nam prik* or sweet chilli sauce as a dip.

Energy 113kcal/468kJ; Protein 5.2g; Carbohydrate 3.6g, of which sugars 3.1g; Fat 8.8g, of which saturates 1.6g, of which polyunsaturates 4g; Cholesterol 95mg; Calcium 56mg; Fibre 2g; Sodium 36mg.

PINEAPPLE WITH GINGER AND CHILLI ★

FRUIT IS OFTEN TREATED LIKE A VEGETABLE AND TOSSED IN A SALAD OR STIR-FRIED. THE PINEAPPLE IS COMBINED WITH THE FLAVOURS OF GINGER AND CHILLI AND SERVED AS A SIDE DISH.

SERVES FOUR

INGREDIENTS

- 15ml/1 tbsp sunflower oil
- 2 garlic cloves, finely shredded
- 40g/1½oz fresh root ginger, peeled and finely shredded
- 2 red Thai chillies, seeded and finely shredded
- 1 pineapple, trimmed, peeled, cored and cut into bitesize chunks
- 15ml/1 tbsp fish sauce
- 30ml/2 tbsp soy sauce
- 15ml–30ml/1–2 tbsp sugar
- 15ml/1 tbsp roasted unsalted peanuts, finely chopped
- 1 lime, cut into quarters, to serve

1 Heat a large wok or heavy pan and add the sunflower oil. Stir in the finely shredded garlic, ginger and chilli. Stir-fry until they begin to colour, then add the pineapple chunks and stir-fry for a further 1–2 minutes, until the edges turn golden.

2 Add the fish sauce, soy sauce and sugar to taste and continue to stir-fry until the pineapple begins to caramelize.

3 Transfer to a serving dish, sprinkle with the roasted peanuts and serve with lime wedges.

Energy 136kcal/577kJ; Protein 2.1g; Carbohydrate 22.8g, of which sugars 22.5g; Fat 4.8g, of which saturates 0.6g, of which polyunsaturates 2.4g; Cholesterol 0mg; Calcium 41mg; Fibre 3g; Sodium 539mg.

FRAGRANT MUSHROOMS IN LETTUCE LEAVES ★

THIS QUICK AND EASY VEGETABLE DISH IS SERVED ON LETTUCE LEAF "SAUCERS" SO IT CAN BE EATEN WITH THE FINGERS, WHICH MAKES IT A GREAT TREAT FOR CHILDREN.

SERVES FOUR

INGREDIENTS

15ml/1 tbsp sunflower oil
2 garlic cloves, finely chopped
2 baby cos or romaine lettuces,
  or 2 Little Gem (Bibb) lettuces
1 lemon grass stalk, finely chopped
2 kaffir lime leaves, rolled in
  cylinders and thinly sliced
200g/7oz/3 cups oyster or chestnut
  mushrooms, sliced
1 small fresh red chilli, seeded
  and finely chopped
juice of ½ lemon
30ml/2 tbsp light soy sauce
5ml/1 tsp palm sugar or light
  muscovado (brown) sugar
small bunch fresh mint, leaves
  removed from the stalks

1 Heat a wok or large, heavy frying pan and add the sunflower oil. Add the finely chopped garlic and cook over a medium heat, stirring occasionally, until golden. Do not let it burn or it will taste bitter.

2 Meanwhile, separate the individual lettuce leaves and set aside.

3 Increase the heat under the wok or pan and add the lemon grass, lime leaves and sliced mushrooms. Stir-fry for about 2 minutes.

4 Add the chilli, lemon juice, soy sauce and sugar to the wok or pan. Toss the mixture over the heat to combine the ingredients together, then stir-fry for a further 2 minutes.

5 Arrange the lettuce leaves on a large plate. Spoon a small amount of the mushroom mixture on to each leaf, top with a mint leaf and serve.

Energy 52kcal/217kJ; Protein 2g; Carbohydrate 3.5g, of which sugars 3.3g; Fat 3.5g, of which saturates 0.5g, of which polyunsaturates 2.1g; Cholesterol 0mg; Calcium 45mg; Fibre 1.8g; Sodium 543mg.

GREEN PAPAYA SALAD ★

AS GREEN PAPAYA IS NOT EASY TO GET HOLD OF, FINELY GRATED CARROTS, CUCUMBER OR EVEN CRISP GREEN APPLE CAN BE USED INSTEAD. ALTERNATIVELY, USE VERY THINLY SLICED WHITE CABBAGE.

SERVES FOUR

INGREDIENTS
1 green papaya
4 garlic cloves, coarsely chopped
15ml/1 tbsp chopped shallots
3–4 fresh red chillies, seeded
  and sliced
2.5ml/½ tsp salt
2–3 snake beans or 6 green beans,
  cut into 2cm/¾ in lengths
2 tomatoes, cut into thin wedges
45ml/3 tbsp Thai fish sauce
15ml/1 tbsp caster (superfine) sugar
juice of 1 lime
15ml/1 tbsp crushed roasted peanuts
sliced fresh red chillies, to garnish

3 Add the sliced snake or green beans and wedges of tomato to the mortar and continue to crush lightly with the pestle until they are incorporated.

4 Season the mixture with the fish sauce, sugar and lime juice. Transfer the salad to a serving dish and sprinkle with the crushed roasted peanuts. Garnish with the sliced red chillies and serve the salad immediately.

1 Cut the papaya in half lengthways. Scrape out the seeds with a spoon and discard, then peel, using a swivel vegetable peeler or a small sharp knife. Shred the flesh finely in a food processor or using a grater.

2 Put the garlic, shallots, red chillies and salt in a large mortar and grind to a paste with a pestle. Add the shredded papaya, pounding with the pestle until it becomes slightly limp and soft.

Energy 68kcal/286kJ; Protein 1.3g; Carbohydrate 15.9g, of which sugars 15.6g; Fat 0.3g, of which saturates 0.1g, of which polyunsaturates 0.1g; Cholesterol 0mg; Calcium 37mg; Fibre 3.1g; Sodium 543mg.

SWEET AND SOUR SALAD ★

THIS REFRESHING SALAD MAKES A PERFECT ACCOMPANIMENT TO A VARIETY OF SPICY DISHES AND CURRIES, WITH ITS CLEAN TASTE AND BRIGHT, JEWEL-LIKE COLOURS, AND POMEGRANATE SEEDS, THOUGH NOT TRADITIONAL, MAKE A BEAUTIFUL GARNISH. THIS IS AN ESSENTIAL DISH FOR A BUFFET PARTY.

SERVES EIGHT

INGREDIENTS
    1 small cucumber
    1 onion, thinly sliced
    1 small, ripe pineapple or 425g/
        15oz can pineapple rings
    1 green (bell) pepper, seeded and
        thinly sliced
    3 firm tomatoes, chopped
    30ml/2 tbsp golden granulated sugar
    45–60ml/3–4 tbsp white wine vinegar
    120ml/4fl oz/1/2 cup water
    salt
    seeds of 1–2 pomegranates,
        to garnish

1 Halve the cucumber lengthways, remove the seeds, slice and spread on a plate with the onion. Sprinkle with salt. After 10 minutes, rinse and dry.

2 If using a fresh pineapple, peel and core it, removing all the eyes, then cut it into bitesize pieces. If using canned pineapple, drain the rings and cut them into small wedges. Place the pineapple in a bowl with the cucumber, onion, green pepper and tomatoes.

3 Heat the sugar, white wine vinegar and measured water in a pan, stirring until the sugar has dissolved. Remove the pan from the heat and leave to cool. When cold, add a little salt to taste and pour over the fruit and vegetables. Cover and chill until required. Serve in small bowls, garnished with pomegranate seeds.

VARIATION
To make an Indonesian-style cucumber salad, salt a salad cucumber as described in the recipe. Make a half quantity of the sugar, vinegar and salt dressing and pour it over the cucumber. Add a few chopped spring onions (scallions). Cover and chill. Serve sprinkled with toasted sesame seeds.

Energy 53kcal/224kJ; Protein 0.9g; Carbohydrate 12.3g, of which sugars 12.1g; Fat 0.3g, of which saturates 0.1g, of which polyunsaturates 0.2g; Cholesterol 0mg; Calcium 20mg; Fibre 1.5g; Sodium 6mg.

THAI FRUIT AND VEGETABLE SALAD ★

THIS FRUIT SALAD IS TRADITIONALLY PRESENTED WITH THE MAIN COURSE AND SERVES AS A COOLER TO COUNTERACT THE HEAT OF THE CHILLIES THAT WILL INEVITABLY BE PRESENT IN THE OTHER DISHES. IT IS A TYPICALLY HARMONIOUS BALANCE OF FLAVOURS.

SERVES SIX

INGREDIENTS

1 small pineapple
1 small mango, peeled and sliced
1 green apple, cored and sliced
6 rambutans or lychees, peeled and
   stoned (pitted)
115g/4oz/1 cup green beans,
   trimmed and halved
1 red onion, sliced
1 small cucumber, cut into
   short sticks
115g/4oz/1⅓ cups beansprouts
2 spring onions (scallions), sliced
1 ripe tomato, quartered
225g/8oz cos, romaine or iceberg
   lettuce leaves
For the coconut dipping sauce
30ml/2 tbsp reduced-fat coconut milk
30ml/2 tbsp granulated sugar
75ml/5 tbsp boiling water
1.5ml/¼ tsp chilli sauce
15ml/1 tbsp Thai fish sauce
juice of 1 lime

1 Make the coconut dipping sauce. Spoon the coconut milk, sugar and boiling water into a screw-top jar. Add the chilli and fish sauces and lime juice, close tightly and shake to mix.

2 Trim both ends of the pineapple with a serrated knife, then cut away the outer skin. Remove the central core with an apple corer. Alternatively, quarter the pineapple lengthways and remove the portion of core from each wedge with a knife. Chop the pineapple and set aside with the other fruits.

3 Bring a small pan of lightly salted water to the boil over a medium heat. Add the green beans and cook for 3–4 minutes, until just tender but still retaining some "bite". Drain, refresh under cold running water, drain well again and set aside.

4 To serve, arrange all the fruits and vegetables in small heaps on a platter or in a shallow bowl. Pour the coconut sauce into a small serving bowl and serve separately as a dip.

Energy 100kcal/425kJ; Protein 2.3g; Carbohydrate 22.6g, of which sugars 21.7g; Fat 0.7g, of which saturates 0.1g, of which polyunsaturates 0.3g; Cholesterol 0mg; Calcium 50mg; Fibre 3.2g; Sodium 190mg.

SOYA BEANSPROUT HERB SALAD ★

HIGH IN VITAMINS, SOYA BEANSPROUTS ARE PARTICULARLY FAVOURED IN SOUTH-EAST ASIA. UNLIKE MUNG BEANSPROUTS, THEY ARE SLIGHTLY POISONOUS WHEN RAW AND NEED TO BE PARBOILED BEFORE USING. TOSSED IN A SALAD, THEY ARE OFTEN EATEN WITH NOODLES AND RICE.

2 Bring a pan of salted water to the boil. Drop in the beansprouts and blanch for a minute only. Drain and refresh under cold water until cool. Drain again and put them into a clean dish towel. Shake out the excess water.

3 Put the beansprouts into a bowl with the spring onions. Pour over the dressing and toss well. Garnish with coriander leaves and serve.

SERVES FOUR

INGREDIENTS
   450g/1lb fresh soya beansprouts
   2 spring onions (scallions), finely
     sliced
   1 small bunch fresh coriander
     (cilantro), stalks removed
For the dressing
   5ml/1 tsp sesame oil
   30ml/2 tbsp fish sauce
   15ml/1 tbsp white rice vinegar
   10ml/2 tsp palm sugar
   1 red chilli, seeded and
     finely sliced
   15g/½oz fresh young root ginger,
     finely shredded

1 First make the dressing. In a bowl, beat the oil, fish sauce and rice vinegar with the sugar, until it dissolves. Stir in the chilli and ginger and leave to stand for 30 minutes to allow the flavours to develop.

Energy 58kcal/245kJ; Protein 3.8g; Carbohydrate 7.9g, of which sugars 5.8g; Fat 1.5g, of which saturates 0.2g, of which polyunsaturates 0.6g; Cholesterol 0mg; Calcium 52mg; Fibre 2.5g; Sodium 11mg.

TABLE SALAD ★

WHEN THIS TABLE SALAD IS SERVED ON ITS OWN, THE VEGETABLES AND FRUIT ARE USUALLY FOLDED INTO LITTLE PACKETS USING LETTUCE LEAVES OR RICE WRAPPERS, AND THEN DIPPED IN A SAUCE, OR ADDED BIT BY BIT TO BOWLS OF RICE OR NOODLES.

SERVES SIX

INGREDIENTS

half a cucumber, peeled and sliced
200g/7oz/scant 1 cup beansprouts
2 carrots, peeled and finely sliced
2 unripe star fruit (carambola), finely sliced
2 green bananas, finely sliced
1 firm papaya, cut in half, seeds removed, peeled and finely sliced
1 bunch each fresh mint and basil, stalks removed
1 crunchy lettuce, leaves separated
juice of 1 lime
dipping sauce, to serve

1 Arrange the cucumber, beansprouts, carrots, star fruit, green bananas, papaya, mint and basil attractively on a large plate. Place the lettuce leaves on one side so that they can be used as wrappers.

2 Squeeze the lime juice over the sliced fruits, particularly the bananas to help them retain their colour, and place the salad in the middle of the table. Serve with a dipping sauce.

Energy 94kcal/397kJ; Protein 2.5g; Carbohydrate 20.6g, of which sugars 11.6g; Fat 0.7g, of which saturates 0.1g, of which polyunsaturates 0.3g; Cholesterol 0mg; Calcium 61mg; Fibre 3.4g; Sodium 14mg.

AUBERGINE SALAD ★

AN APPETIZING AND UNUSUAL SALAD THAT YOU WILL FIND YOURSELF MAKING OVER AND OVER AGAIN. ROASTING THE AUBERGINES REALLY BRINGS OUT THEIR FLAVOUR.

SERVES SIX

INGREDIENTS
2 aubergines (eggplant)
15ml/1 tbsp sunflower oil
30ml/2 tbsp dried shrimp, soaked in warm water for 10 minutes
15ml/1 tbsp coarsely chopped garlic
1 hard-boiled egg, chopped
4 shallots, thinly sliced into rings
fresh coriander (cilantro) leaves and 2 fresh red chillies, seeded and sliced, to garnish
For the dressing
30ml/2 tbsp fresh lime juice
5ml/1 tsp palm sugar or light muscovado (brown) sugar
30ml/2 tbsp Thai fish sauce

1 Preheat the grill (broiler) to medium or preheat the oven to 180°C/350°F/ Gas 4. Prick the aubergines several times with a skewer, then arrange on a baking sheet. Cook them under the grill for 30–40 minutes, or until they are charred and tender. Alternatively, roast them by placing them directly on the shelf of the oven for about 1 hour, turning them at least twice. Remove the aubergines and set aside until they are cool enough to handle.

2 Meanwhile, make the dressing. Put the lime juice, palm or muscovado sugar and fish sauce into a small bowl. Whisk well with a fork or balloon whisk. Cover with clear film (plastic wrap) and set aside until required.

3 When the aubergines are cool enough to handle, peel off the skin and cut the flesh into medium slices.

4 Heat the oil in a small frying pan. Drain the dried shrimp thoroughly and add them to the pan with the garlic. Cook over a medium heat for about 3 minutes, until golden. Remove from the pan and set aside.

5 Arrange the aubergine slices on a serving dish. Top with the hard-boiled egg, shallots and dried shrimp mixture. Drizzle over the dressing and garnish with the coriander and red chillies.

VARIATION
For a special occasion, use salted duck's or quail's eggs, cut in half, instead of chopped hen's eggs.

Energy 61kcal/254kJ; Protein 4.8g; Carbohydrate 3.6g, of which sugars 2.8g; Fat 3.2g, of which saturates 0.6g, of which polyunsaturates 1.5g; Cholesterol 57mg; Calcium 75mg; Fibre 1.6g; Sodium 408mg.

CABBAGE SALAD ★

THIS IS A SIMPLE AND DELICIOUS WAY OF SERVING A SOMEWHAT MUNDANE VEGETABLE. CLASSIC THAI FLAVOURS OF CHILLI AND PEANUTS PERMEATE THIS COLOURFUL WARM SALAD.

SERVES SIX

INGREDIENTS
  15ml/1 tbsp sunflower oil
  2 large fresh red chillies, seeded
    and cut into thin strips
  6 garlic cloves, thinly sliced
  6 shallots, thinly sliced
  1 small cabbage, shredded
  15ml/1 tbsp coarsely chopped
    roasted peanuts, to garnish
For the dressing
  30ml/2 tbsp Thai fish sauce
  grated rind of 1 lime
  30ml/2 tbsp fresh lime juice
  120ml/4fl oz/½ cup reduced-fat
    coconut milk

VARIATION
Cauliflower and broccoli can also be
cooked in this way.

1 Make the dressing by mixing the fish sauce, lime rind and juice and coconut milk in a bowl. Whisk until thoroughly combined, then set aside.

2 Heat the oil in a wok. Stir-fry the chillies, garlic and shallots over a medium heat for 3–4 minutes, until the shallots are brown and crisp. Remove with a slotted spoon and set aside.

3 Bring a large pan of lightly salted water to the boil. Add the cabbage and blanch for 2–3 minutes. Tip it into a colander, drain well and put into a bowl.

4 Whisk the dressing again, add it to the warm cabbage and toss to mix. Transfer the salad to a serving dish. Sprinkle with the fried shallot mixture and the peanuts. Serve immediately.

Energy 70kcal/290kJ; Protein 2.2g; Carbohydrate 8.3g, of which sugars 7g; Fat 3.3g, of which saturates 0.5g, of which polyunsaturates 1.6g; Cholesterol 0mg; Calcium 51mg; Fibre 2.2g; Sodium 206mg.

POMELO AND CRAB SALAD ★

TYPICALLY, A THAI MEAL INCLUDES A SELECTION OF ABOUT FIVE DISHES, ONE OF WHICH IS OFTEN A REFRESHING AND PALATE-CLEANSING SALAD THAT FEATURES TROPICAL FRUIT.

SERVES SIX

INGREDIENTS
  15ml/1 tbsp sunflower oil
  4 shallots, finely sliced
  2 garlic cloves, finely sliced
  1 large pomelo
  15ml/1 tbsp roasted peanuts
  115g/4oz cooked peeled
    prawns (shrimp)
  115g/4oz cooked crab meat
  10–12 small fresh mint leaves
For the dressing
  30ml/2 tbsp Thai fish sauce
  15ml/1 tbsp palm sugar or light
    muscovado (brown) sugar
  30ml/2 tbsp fresh lime juice
For the garnish
  2 spring onions (scallions),
    thinly sliced
  2 fresh red chillies, seeded and
    thinly sliced
  fresh coriander (cilantro) leaves
  shredded fresh coconut (optional)

1 Make the dressing. Mix the fish sauce, sugar and lime juice in a bowl. Whisk well, then cover with clear film (plastic wrap) and set aside.

2 Heat the oil in a small frying pan, add the shallots and garlic and cook over a medium heat until they are golden. Remove from the pan and set aside.

3 Peel the pomelo and break the flesh into small pieces, taking care to remove any membranes.

4 Grind the peanuts coarsely and put them in a salad bowl. Add the pomelo flesh, prawns, crab meat, mint leaves and the shallot mixture. Pour over the dressing, toss lightly and sprinkle with the spring onions, chillies and coriander leaves. Add the shredded coconut, if using. Serve immediately.

COOK'S TIP
The pomelo is a large citrus fruit that looks rather like a grapefruit, although it is not, as is sometimes thought, a hybrid. It is slightly pear-shaped with thick, yellow, dimpled skin and pinkish-yellow flesh that is both sturdier and drier than that of a grapefruit. It also has a sharper taste. Pomelos are sometimes known as "shaddocks" after the sea captain who brought them from their native Polynesia to the Caribbean.

SEAFOOD SALAD <u>WITH</u> FRAGRANT HERBS ★★

THIS IS A SPECTACULAR SALAD. THE LUSCIOUS COMBINATION OF PRAWNS, SCALLOPS AND SQUID MAKES IT THE IDEAL CHOICE FOR A SPECIAL CELEBRATION.

SERVES FOUR TO SIX

INGREDIENTS

- 250ml/8fl oz/1 cup fish stock or water
- 350g/12oz squid, cleaned and cut into rings
- 12 raw king prawns (jumbo shrimp), peeled, with tails intact
- 12 scallops
- 50g/2oz cellophane noodles, soaked in warm water for 30 minutes
- ½ cucumber, cut into thin batons
- 1 lemon grass stalk, finely chopped
- 2 kaffir lime leaves, finely shredded
- 2 shallots, thinly sliced
- 30ml/2 tbsp chopped spring onions (scallions)
- 30ml/2 tbsp fresh coriander (cilantro) leaves
- 12–15 fresh mint leaves, coarsely torn
- 4 fresh red chillies, seeded and cut into slivers
- juice of 1–2 limes
- 30ml/2 tbsp Thai fish sauce
- fresh coriander sprigs, to garnish

1 Pour the fish stock or water into a medium pan, set over a high heat and bring to the boil. Cook each type of seafood separately in the stock for 3–4 minutes. Remove with a slotted spoon and set aside to cool.

2 Drain the noodles. Using scissors, cut them into short lengths, about 5cm/2in long. Place them in a serving bowl and add the cucumber, lemon grass, kaffir lime leaves, shallots, spring onions, coriander, mint and chillies.

3 Pour over the lime juice and fish sauce. Mix well, then add the seafood. Toss lightly. Garnish with the fresh coriander sprigs and serve.

Energy 339kcal/1420kJ; Protein 27.3g; Carbohydrate 42g, of which sugars 2.3g; Fat 6.8g, of which saturates 0.9g, of which polyunsaturates 3.2g; Cholesterol 219mg; Calcium 148mg; Fibre 1.7g; Sodium 861mg.

SHRIMP, PINEAPPLE AND CUCMBER SALAD ★

THIS SPICY LITTLE SIDE DISH MAKES A GREAT ACCOMPANIMENT TO ANY RICE-BASED MEAL. THE COMBINATION OF THE PINEAPPLE AND CUCUMBER MIXES WELL WITH THE CHILLI.

SERVES TEN

INGREDIENTS
    1 small or ¹/₂ large fresh
      ripe pineapple
    ¹/₂ cucumber, halved lengthways
    50g/2oz dried shrimps
    1 large fresh red chilli, seeded
    1cm/¹/₂in cube shrimp paste,
      prepared (see Cook's Tip)
    juice of 1 large lemon or lime
    light brown sugar, to taste (optional)

1 Cut off both ends of the pineapple. Stand it upright on a board, then slice off the skin from top to bottom, cutting out the spines. Slice the pineapple, removing the central core. Cut into thin slices and set aside.

2 Trim the ends from the cucumber and slice thinly. Sprinkle with salt and set aside. Place the dried shrimps in a food processor and chop fairly finely. Add the chilli, prepared shrimp paste and lemon or lime juice and process again to a paste.

3 Rinse the cucumber, drain and dry on kitchen paper.

4 Mix the cucumber with the pineapple and chill. Just before serving, spoon in the spice mixture with sugar to taste. Mix well and serve.

COOK'S TIP
The pungent shrimp paste, is popular in many South-east Asian countries, and is available in Asian supermarkets. Since it can taste a bit raw in a sambal, dry fry it by wrapping in foil and heating in a frying pan over a low heat for 5 minutes, turning from time to time. If the shrimp paste is to be fried with other spices, this preliminary cooking can be eliminated.

Energy 48kcal/203kJ; Protein 3.2g; Carbohydrate 8.6g, of which sugars 8.5g; Fat 0.3g, of which saturates 0g, of which polyunsaturates 0.1g; Cholesterol 25mg; Calcium 77mg; Fibre 1.1g; Sodium 219mg.

CHICKEN AND SHREDDED CABBAGE SALAD ★

CHICKEN IS OFTEN COOKED WHOLE IN WATER WITH HERBS AND FLAVOURINGS. THE CHICKEN IS THEN SHREDDED. SOME OF THE MEAT GOES BACK INTO THE BROTH, THE REST IS TOSSED IN A SALAD.

SERVES SIX

INGREDIENTS
   450g/1lb chicken, cooked and torn
      into thin strips
   1 white Chinese cabbage, trimmed
      and finely shredded
   2 carrots, finely shredded
      or grated
   a small bunch fresh mint, stalks
      removed, finely shredded
   1 small bunch fresh coriander
      (cilantro) leaves, to garnish
For the dressing
   15ml/1 tbsp sunflower oil
   30ml/2 tbsp white rice vinegar
   45ml/3 tbsp fish sauce
   juice of 2 limes
   30ml/2 tbsp palm sugar
   2 red Thai chillies, seeded and
      finely chopped
   25g/1oz fresh young root
      ginger, sliced
   3 garlic cloves, crushed
   2 shallots, finely chopped

1 First make the dressing. In a bowl, beat the oil, vinegar, fish sauce and lime juice with the sugar, until it has dissolved. Stir in the other ingredients and leave to stand for about 30 minutes to let the flavours mingle.

2 Put the cooked chicken strips, cabbage, carrots and mint in a large bowl. Pour over the dressing and toss well. Garnish with coriander leaves and serve.

Energy 170kcal/715kJ; Protein 20.4g; Carbohydrate 15.8g, of which sugars 13.7g; Fat 3.1g, of which saturates 0.5g, of which polyunsaturates 1.5g; Cholesterol 53mg; Calcium 94mg; Fibre 3.2g; Sodium 60mg.

DESSERTS

After a meal, it is customary to serve a simple platter of freshly sliced fruits, usually watermelon and orange segments, to refresh and cleanse the palate. Of course, you can serve up any fruits you like — mangoes, pears, pineapples and bananas will work just as well — but if you're looking for something extra special, try fragrant Papayas in Jasmine Flower Syrup, or sweet and sticky Coconut Custard.

COCONUT ICE CREAM ★

ICE CREAM MADE WITH COCONUT MILK AND CONDENSED MILK CAN BE HIGH IN FAT, BUT IN THIS LOW-FAT RECIPE, REDUCED-FAT IS USED TO MAKE THIS RECIPE SUITABLE FOR A LOW-FAT DIETS.

2 Pour the mixture into the frozen freezer bowl of an ice-cream maker (or follow the appliance instructions) and churn till the mixture has thickened. (This will take 30–40 minutes.)

3 Transfer the mixture to a lidded plastic tub, cover and freeze until the consistency is right for scooping. If you do not have an ice-cream maker, pour the mixture into a shallow container and freeze on the coldest setting.

4 When ice crystals form around the sides of the ice cream, beat the mixture, then return it to the freezer. Do this at least twice. The more you do it, the creamier the mixture will be.

5 Make the sauce. Mix the sugar, measured water and ginger in a pan. Stir over medium heat until the sugar has dissolved, then bring the liquid to the boil. Add the pandan leaf, if using, tying it into a knot so that it can easily be removed with the ginger before serving. Lower the heat and simmer for 3–4 minutes. Set aside till required.

6 Serve the ice cream in coconut shells or in a bowl. Sprinkle with the strips of coconut and serve with the gula melaka sauce, which can be hot, warm or cold.

SERVES SIX

INGREDIENTS
   400ml/14fl oz can reduced-fat
     coconut milk
   400ml/14fl oz can reduced-fat
     condensed milk
   2.5ml/1/2 tsp salt
For the sauce
   150g/5oz/3/4 cup palm sugar or
     muscovado (molasses) sugar
   150ml/1/4 pint/2/3 cup water
   1cm/1/2in slice fresh root
     ginger, bruised
   1 pandan leaf (if available)
   coconut shells (optional) and thinly
     pared strips of coconut, to serve

1 Chill the cans of coconut and condensed milk very thoroughly. In a bowl, mix the coconut milk with the condensed milk. Gently whisk together with the salt.

COOK'S TIP
Coconut milk takes longer to freeze than double (heavy) cream, so allow plenty of time for the process.

Energy 291kcal/1242kJ; Protein 7g; Carbohydrate 69.4g, of which sugars 69.4g; Fat 0.3g, of which saturates 0.2g, of which polyunsaturates 0g; Cholesterol 1mg; Calcium 253mg; Fibre 0g; Sodium 175mg.

EXOTIC FRUIT SALAD WITH PASSION FRUIT ★

PASSION FRUIT MAKES A SUPERB DRESSING FOR ANY FRUIT, BUT REALLY BRINGS OUT THE FLAVOUR OF EXOTIC VARIETIES. YOU CAN EASILY DOUBLE THE RECIPE, THEN SERVE THE REST FOR BREAKFAST.

SERVES SIX

INGREDIENTS
   1 mango
   1 papaya
   2 kiwi fruit
   reduced-fat coconut or vanilla ice
     cream, to serve
For the dressing
   3 passion fruit
   thinly pared rind and juice of 1 lime
   5ml/1 tsp hazelnut or walnut oil
   15ml/1 tbsp clear honey

COOK'S TIP
Clear honey scented with orange blossom would be perfect for the dressing.

1 Peel the mango, cut it into three slices, then cut the flesh into chunks and place it in a large bowl. Peel the papaya and cut it in half. Scoop out the seeds, then chop the flesh.

2 Cut both ends off each kiwi fruit, then stand them on a board. Using a small sharp knife, cut off the skin from top to bottom. Cut each kiwi fruit in half lengthways, then cut into thick slices. Combine all the fruit in a large bowl.

3 Make the dressing. Cut each passion fruit in half and scoop the seeds out into a sieve set over a small bowl. Press the seeds well to extract all their juices. Lightly whisk the remaining dressing ingredients into the passion fruit juice, then pour the dressing over the fruit. Mix gently to combine. Leave to chill for 1 hour before serving with scoops of coconut or vanilla ice cream.

Energy 66kcal/278kJ; Protein 1g; Carbohydrate 14.6g, of which sugars 14.5g; Fat 0.8g, of which saturates 0.1g, of which polyunsaturates 0.4g; Cholesterol 0mg; Calcium 26mg; Fibre 2.9g; Sodium 7mg.

PAPAYAS IN JASMINE FLOWER SYRUP ★

THE FRAGRANT SYRUP CAN BE PREPARED IN ADVANCE, USING FRESH JASMINE FLOWERS FROM A HOUSE PLANT OR THE GARDEN. IT TASTES FABULOUS WITH PAPAYAS, BUT IT IS ALSO GOOD WITH ALL SORTS OF DESSERTS. TRY IT WITH ICE CREAM OR SPOONED OVER LYCHEES OR MANGOES.

SERVES TWO

INGREDIENTS
105ml/7 tbsp water
45ml/3 tbsp palm sugar or light muscovado (brown) sugar
20–30 jasmine flowers, plus a few extra flowers, to decorate (optional)
2 ripe papayas
juice of 1 lime

COOK'S TIP
Although scented white jasmine flowers are perfectly safe to eat, it is important to make certain that the flowers have not been sprayed with pesticides or any other harmful chemicals. Washing the flowers will not necessarily remove all the residue.

1 Place the water and sugar in a small pan. Heat gently, stirring occasionally, until the sugar has dissolved, then simmer, without stirring, over a low heat for 4 minutes.

2 Pour into a bowl, leave to cool slightly, then add the jasmine flowers. Leave to steep for at least 20 minutes.

3 Peel the papayas and slice in half lengthways. Scoop out and discard the seeds. Place the papayas on serving plates and squeeze over the lime.

4 Strain the syrup into a clean bowl, discarding the flowers. Spoon the syrup over the papayas. If you like, decorate with a few fresh jasmine flowers.

Energy 197kcal/837kJ; Protein 1.6g; Carbohydrate 49.9g, of which sugars 49.9g; Fat 0.3g, of which saturates 0g, of which polyunsaturates 0g; Cholesterol 0mg; Calcium 81mg; Fibre 6.6g; Sodium 17mg.

COCONUT CREAM DIAMONDS ★

DESSERTS LIKE THESE ARE SERVED IN COUNTRIES ALL OVER ASIA, OFTEN WITH MANGOES, PINEAPPLE OR GUAVAS. ALTHOUGH COMMERCIALLY GROUND RICE CAN BE USED FOR THIS DISH, GRINDING JASMINE RICE YOURSELF — IN A FOOD PROCESSOR — GIVES A MUCH BETTER RESULT.

SERVES SIX

INGREDIENTS

   75g/3oz/scant ½ cup jasmine rice,
     soaked overnight in 175ml/6fl oz/
     ¾ cup water
   350ml/12fl oz/1½ cups reduced-fat
     coconut milk
   150ml/¼ pint/⅔ cup reduced-fat
     single (light) cream
   50g/2oz/¼ cup caster
     (superfine) sugar
   raspberries and fresh mint leaves,
     to decorate
For the coulis
   75g/3oz/¾ cup blackcurrants,
     stalks removed
   30ml/2 tbsp caster (superfine) sugar
   75g/3oz/½ cup fresh or
     frozen raspberries

1 Put the rice and its soaking water into a food processor and process for a few minutes until the mixture is soupy.

2 Heat the coconut milk and cream in a non-stick pan. When the mixture is on the point of boiling, stir in the rice mixture. Cook over a very gentle heat for 10 minutes, stirring constantly.

3 Stir the sugar into the coconut rice mixture and continue cooking for a further 10–15 minutes, or until the mixture is thick and creamy.

VARIATION

You could use other soft fruit in the coulis, such as blackberries or redcurrants.

4 Line a rectangular tin (pan) with baking parchment. Pour the coconut rice mixture into the pan, cool, then chill in the refrigerator until the dessert is set and firm.

5 Meanwhile, make the coulis. Put the blackcurrants in a bowl and sprinkle with the sugar. Set aside for about 30 minutes. Tip the blackcurrants and raspberries into a wire sieve set over a bowl. Using a spoon, press the fruit against the sides of the sieve so that the juices collect in the bowl. Taste the coulis and add more sugar if necessary.

6 Carefully cut the coconut cream into diamonds. Spoon a little of the coulis on to each dessert plate, arrange the coconut cream diamonds on top and decorate with the fresh raspberries and mint leaves. Serve immediately.

Energy 146kcal/616kJ; Protein 2g; Carbohydrate 28.5g, of which sugars 18.5g; Fat 3.1g, of which saturates 2g, of which polyunsaturates 0.1g; Cholesterol 8mg; Calcium 50mg; Fibre 0.8g; Sodium 70mg.

TROPICAL FRUIT GRATIN ★★

THIS OUT-OF-THE-ORDINARY GRATIN IS STRICTLY FOR GROWN-UPS. A COLOURFUL COMBINATION OF FRUIT IS TOPPED WITH A SIMPLE SABAYON BEFORE BEING FLASHED UNDER THE GRILL.

SERVES FOUR

INGREDIENTS
  2 tamarillos
  ½ sweet pineapple
  1 ripe mango
  175g/6oz/1½ cups blackberries
  120ml/4fl oz/½ cup sparkling
    white wine
  115g/4oz/½ cup caster
    (superfine) sugar
  6 egg yolks

VARIATIONS
• If making this gratin for children, replace the wine with orange, white grape or pineapple juice.
• If tamarillos are not available in your supermarket, use bananas instead.

1 Cut each tamarillo in half lengthways, then into thick slices. Cut the rind and core from the pineapple and take spiral slices off the outside to remove the eyes. Cut the flesh into chunks. Peel the mango, cut it in half and cut the flesh from the stone (pit) in slices.

2 Divide all the fruit, including the blackberries, among four 14cm/5½in gratin dishes set on a baking sheet and set aside. Heat the wine and sugar in a pan until the sugar has dissolved. Bring to the boil and cook for 5 minutes.

3 Put the egg yolks in a large heatproof bowl. Place the bowl over a pan of simmering water and whisk until pale. Slowly pour on the hot sugar syrup, whisking all the time, until the mixture thickens. Preheat the grill (broiler).

4 Spoon the mixture over the fruit. Place the baking sheet holding the dishes on a low shelf under the hot grill until the topping is golden. Serve the gratin hot.

GRILLED PINEAPPLE WITH PAPAYA SAUCE ★

PINEAPPLE AND STEM GINGER IS A CLASSIC COMBINATION. WHEN COOKED IN THIS WAY, THE FRUIT TAKES ON A SUPERB FLAVOUR AND IS SIMPLY SENSATIONAL WHEN SERVED WITH THE PAPAYA SAUCE.

SERVES SIX

INGREDIENTS
  1 sweet pineapple
  melted butter, for greasing
    and brushing
  2 pieces drained stem ginger in
    syrup, cut into fine matchsticks,
    plus 30ml/2 tbsp of the syrup
    from the jar
  30ml/2 tbsp demerara (raw) sugar
  pinch of ground cinnamon
  fresh mint sprigs, to decorate
For the sauce
  1 ripe papaya, peeled and seeded
  175ml/6fl oz/¾ cup apple juice

1 Peel the pineapple and take spiral slices off the outside to remove the eyes. Cut it crossways into six slices, each 2.5cm/1in thick. Line a baking sheet with a sheet of foil, rolling up the sides to make a rim. Grease the foil with melted butter. Preheat the grill (broiler).

2 Arrange the pineapple slices on the lined baking sheet. Brush with butter, then top with the ginger matchsticks, sugar and cinnamon. Drizzle over the stem ginger syrup. Grill (broil) for 5–7 minutes or until the slices are golden and lightly charred on top.

3 Meanwhile, make the sauce. Cut a few slices from the papaya and set aside, then purée the rest with the apple juice in a blender or food processor.

4 Press the purée through a sieve placed over a bowl, then stir in any juices from cooking the pineapple. Serve the pineapple slices with a little sauce drizzled around each plate. Decorate with the reserved papaya slices and the mint sprigs.

COOK'S TIP
Try the papaya sauce with savoury dishes, too. It tastes great with grilled chicken and game birds as well as pork and lamb.

Top: Energy 300kcal/1270kJ; Protein 6.2g; Carbohydrate 52.8g, of which sugars 52.7g; Fat 8.7g, of which saturates 2.4g, of which polyunsaturates 1.1g; Cholesterol 302mg; Calcium 119mg; Fibre 4.6g; Sodium 22mg.
Bottom: Energy 97kcal/415kJ; Protein 0.7g; Carbohydrate 24.7g, of which sugars 24.7g; Fat 0.2g, of which saturates 0g, of which polyunsaturates 0.1g; Cholesterol 0mg; Calcium 33mg; Fibre 2.3g; Sodium 19mg.

COCONUT CUSTARD ★★

THIS TRADITIONAL DESSERT CAN BE BAKED OR STEAMED AND IS OFTEN SERVED WITH SWEET STICKY RICE AND A SELECTION OF FRESH FRUIT. MANGOES AND TAMARILLOS COMBINE VERY WELL.

2 Strain the mixture into a jug (pitcher), then pour it into four individual heatproof glasses, ramekins or an ovenproof dish.

3 Stand the glasses, ramekins or dish in a roasting pan. Fill the pan with hot water to reach halfway up the sides of the ramekins or dish.

4 Bake for about 35–40 minutes, or until the custards are set. Test with a fine skewer or cocktail stick (toothpick).

5 Remove the roasting pan from the oven, lift out the ramekins or dish and leave to cool.

6 If you like, turn out the custards on to serving plate(s). Decorate with the mint leaves and a dusting of icing sugar, and serve with sliced fruit.

SERVES FOUR

INGREDIENTS
  4 eggs
  75g/3oz/6 tbsp soft light
    muscovado (brown) sugar
    or palm sugar
  250ml/8fl oz/1 cup reduced-fat
    coconut milk
  5ml/1 tsp vanilla, rose or
    jasmine extract
  fresh mint leaves and icing
    (confectioners') sugar,
    to decorate
  sliced fruit, to serve

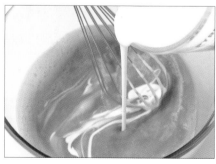

1 Preheat the oven to 150°C/300°F/ Gas 2. Whisk the eggs and sugar in a bowl until smooth. Add the coconut milk and extract and whisk well.

Energy 161kcal/681kJ; Protein 6.5g; Carbohydrate 22.7g, of which sugars 22.7g; Fat 5.7g, of which saturates 1.7g, of which polyunsaturates 0.6g; Cholesterol 190mg; Calcium 57mg; Fibre 0g; Sodium 140mg.

TAPIOCA PUDDING ★

THIS PUDDING, MADE FROM LARGE PEARL TAPIOCA AND COCONUT MILK AND SERVED WARM, IS MUCH LIGHTER THAN THE WESTERN-STYLE VERSION. YOU CAN ADJUST THE SWEETNESS TO YOUR TASTE.

SERVES FOUR

INGREDIENTS

115g/4oz/⅔ cup tapioca
475ml/16fl oz/2 cups water
175g/6oz/¾ cup granulated sugar
pinch of salt
250ml/8fl oz/1 cup reduced-fat
  coconut milk
250g/9oz prepared tropical fruits,
  such as lychees and papayas
finely shredded lime rind
  and shavings of fresh coconut
  (optional), to decorate

1 Put the tapioca in a bowl and pour over warm water to cover. Leave to soak for 1 hour so the grains swell. Drain.

2 Pour the measured water in a large pan and bring to the boil over a medium heat. Add the sugar and salt and stir until dissolved.

3 Add the tapioca and coconut milk, reduce the heat to low and simmer gently for 10 minutes, or until the tapioca becomes transparent.

4 Spoon into one large or four individual bowls and serve warm with the tropical fruits. Decorate with the lime rind and coconut shavings, if using.

Energy 324kcal/1384kJ; Protein 1g; Carbohydrate 84.7g, of which sugars 57.2g; Fat 0.4g, of which saturates 0.2g, of which polyunsaturates 0g; Cholesterol 0mg; Calcium 51mg; Fibre 1.8g; Sodium 74mg.

PASTRY FRITTERS ★

THESE IRRESISTIBLE FRITTERS, SERVED AT EVERY OPPORTUNITY WITH HOT CHOCOLATE OR COFFEE,
CAME TO THE PHILIPPINES WITH THE SPANISH WHO WERE KEEN TO KEEP MEMORIES OF HOME ALIVE.

MAKES ABOUT TWENTY-FOUR

INGREDIENTS
450ml/15fl oz/scant 2 cups water
15ml/1 tbsp olive oil
15ml/1 tbsp sugar, plus extra
   for sprinkling
2.5ml/1/2 tsp salt
150g/5oz/11/4 cups plain
   (all-purpose) flour
1 large (US extra large) egg
sunflower oil, for deep-frying
caster (superfine) sugar,
   for sprinkling

COOK'S TIP
If you don't have a piping (pastry) bag,
you could fry teaspoons of mixture in
the same way. Don't try to fry too many
fritters at a time as they swell a little
during cooking.

1 Mix the water, oil, sugar and salt in a
large pan and bring to the boil. Remove
from the heat, and then sift in the
flour. Beat well with a wooden spoon
until smooth.

2 Beat in the egg to make a smooth,
glossy mixture with a piping consistency.
Spoon into a piping (pastry) bag fitted
with a large star nozzle.

3 Heat the oil in a wok or deep fryer to
190°C/375°F. Pipe loops of the mixture,
two at a time, into the hot oil. Cook
the loops for 3–4 minutes until they
are golden.

4 Lift out the fritters with a wire
skimmer or slotted spoon and drain
them on kitchen paper. Dredge them
with caster sugar and serve warm.

SWEET CARAMEL FLAN ★

SERVE THIS TRADITIONAL DESSERT HOT OR COLD WITH CHILLED YOGURT. EVAPORATED MILK
IS OFTEN USED AS A SWEETENER FOR DESSERTS AND STEAMED BREADS.

SERVES EIGHT

INGREDIENTS
5 large eggs
30ml/2 tbsp caster (superfine) sugar
few drops vanilla extract
410g/141/2oz can reduced-fat
   evaporated (unsweetened
   condensed) milk
300ml/1/2 pint/11/4 cups skimmed milk
5ml/1 tsp finely grated lime rind
strips of lime rind, to decorate
For the caramel
225g/8oz/1 cup sugar
120ml/4fl oz/1/2 cup water

1 Make the caramel. Put the sugar and
water in a heavy pan. Stir to dissolve
the sugar, then boil without stirring
until golden. Pour into eight ramekins,
rotating to coat the sides.

2 Preheat the oven to 150°C/300°F/
Gas 2. Beat the eggs, sugar and vanilla
extract in a bowl. Mix the evaporated
milk and fresh milk in a pan. Heat to
just below boiling point, then pour on
to the egg mixture, stirring all the time.
Strain the custard mixture into a jug,
add the grated lime rind and cool. Pour
into the caramel-coated ramekins.

3 Place the ramekins in a roasting pan
and pour in enough warm water to come
halfway up the sides of the dishes.

4 Transfer the roasting pan to the oven
and cook the custards for 35–45
minutes or until they just shimmer when
the ramekins are gently shaken.

5 Serve the custards in their ramekin
dishes or by inverting on to serving
plates, in which case break the caramel
and use as decoration. The custards
can be served warm or cold, decorated
with strips of lime rind.

COOK'S TIP
Make extra caramel, if you like, for a
garnish. Pour on to lightly oiled foil and
leave to set, then crush with a rolling pin.

Top: Energy 62kcal/257kJ; Protein 0.9g; Carbohydrate 5.7g, of which sugars 0.9g; Fat 4.1g, of which saturates 0.5g, of which polyunsaturates 2.2g; Cholesterol 8mg; Calcium 10mg; Fibre 0.2g; Sodium 3mg.
Bottom: Energy 320kcal/1361kJ; Protein 10.5g; Carbohydrate 65.7g, of which sugars 65.7g; Fat 3.7g, of which saturates 1.1g, of which polyunsaturates 0.4g; Cholesterol 121mg; Calcium 250mg; Fibre 0g; Sodium 139mg.

INDEX